# MAN ON A ROCK

# MAN ON A ROCK

*By* RICHARD HERTZ

CHAPEL HILL
The University of North Carolina Press

Copyright, 1946, by
The University of North Carolina Press

Printed in the United States of America by
VAN REES PRESS · NEW YORK · PJ

TO THE MEMORY OF MY FRIEND

## RUDOLF VON SCHELIHA

who, braver than I, remained in Germany and, like many of my friends and former colleagues in the German Foreign Office, died gloriously on Hitler's gallows.

# Acknowledgment

I am grateful to Mr. W. T. Couch—formerly Director of The University of North Carolina Press, now Director of The University of Chicago Press—for his interest and help. Without his aid this essay in idealism might never have seen the light of an American day in presentable shape.

R. H.

# CONTENTS

Introduction: Salas y Gomez    1

I: The Middle Class and Europe    19

II: Birth and Death of the Spirit    58

III: The Revival of the Spirit Fails    105

IV: Utopias without Spirit    131

V: The Century of the Common Man    161

Notes    179

# MAN ON A ROCK

*For perfect contemplation we require bodily health, which is secured by all such artificial contrivances as are necessary to life. We require freedom from the perturbation of the passions—a goal attained by the moral virtues and by prudence. We require freedom from external perturbations—a freedom at which the entire organization of civil government aims. So, if you look at the matter rightly, all human occupations appear to be directed to the needs of those who contemplate the Truth.*

—St. Thomas Aquinas

INTRODUCTION:

# SALAS Y GOMEZ

> *We live to stand alone, and listen to the Holy Ghost.*
> —D. H. LAWRENCE

IT SO HAPPENED THAT THE POET CHAMISSO GREW UP IN France, surrounded by the chalky hills of the Champagne; the evergreen arbours in the garden of the castle Boncourt where he was born were powdered by a fine white dust, and so were the vineyards beyond the solid stone fence which protected his first steps and his first illusions. Being an aristocrat, and thus unwittingly embodying memories which were mild to him but oppressive, perhaps, to his less prominent neighbours, he had to flee to foreign lands before the fury of the French Revolution. He found asylum in the ascetic plains of Prussia and became an officer in the Prussian army. In 1813, however, when his new fatherland turned with great patriotic fervor against the formidable Napoleon, Chamisso could not bring himself to bear arms against France. He retired to a solitary manor house belonging to a count with the unorthodox name of Itzenplitz, and there he wrote the story of the man without a shadow—Peter Schlemihl.

Peter Schlemihl was looking for his shadow and could not find it. Cosmopolitans beware! Like Chamisso, Schlemihl lacked something essential. He was a marked man. Wherever he went people soon discovered that he stood not quite on his feet, that his constitution had an alien rhythm, that he did not belong; that, without a shadow, he was himself a shadow of happier and more normal beings. Schlemihl's whole life was taken up with pretending that he was like everybody else.

Chamisso of course described his own situation. He could not drink from the same emotional sources as did the man in the street and the man in the field. The patriotic suggestions of this legend and that monument were lost on him. The national destiny which moved the other actors in the puppet show of history did not move him. The rites which transformed a crowd of selfish and indifferent men into an enthusiastic brotherhood did not concern him. He was estranged, alone with his poor self and the vagaries of unconnected and unintegrated thoughts.

The intoxicating cup of tribal emotions thus passed Chamisso's lips, and while the victory bells in the village church rang to the initiated with a majestic significance, he shrank from this turbulent profession of loyalty into the emptiness of his unrelated heart. Unsupported by the *esprit de corps* of an aroused people, he classified bugs and minerals behind drawn curtains. The silence of the night was like the withdrawal of a guiding hand. And yet, and yet, this story of an abandoned soul is not the whole story.

Chamisso wrote a poem, *Salas y Gomez*. Here another kind of relationship balances and supersedes the abandonment of men without country. The emptiness is filled again, not with bugs and minerals, but with the slow emergence of a virgin continent of the spirit, with its own loyalties, its own monuments, and its own victory bells. A consciousness, forced to look beyond the picturesque follies of the tribe, sinks back into the arms of the cosmos.

In *Salas y Gomez* we hear of a young man who sails into the wide world, his imagination generously stocked with dreams of worldly renown and affluence. In the inhospitable vastness of the Pacific his ship foundered, however, and as chance would have it, our hero alone was washed ashore upon a small, bare rock, a piece of creation in the negative, a long litany of fiasco. On this petrified curse he spent a solitary half century or more, sustained by the eggs of innumerable, stupidly agitated, and screeching birds. He was dying when he was found "nude, wrapped down to the loins in the silver of his beard... quiet in his rigid face." Near him were three slates covered with an account of his experiences.

It was a bitter fate, no doubt, which this involuntary hermit related on the slates. He was face to face with nothing but time, and a dwindling hope. Once he was mocked by a ship which cruised around the rock and filled him for a moment with a mad anticipation of that fullness of life which he was condemned to miss; but the ship did not notice his ineffectual signals, and sailed on. An Alexander in reverse, he did not cry for worlds to conquer, he wanted to be reconquered by the world. For years, we may assume, he could not find himself because there was nobody to supply a measure. Here was a potential Napoleon or Shakespeare, or a potential burgomaster or a potential grocer or a potential scoundrel, walking over the porous, sun-drenched cliffs; but to the birds and fish he was another cloud or wave, a moving object in an existence dizzy with moving objects; as an individual he was forced into the absolute, and therefore obliterated.

The poor man was even prevented from exercising his social talents for his own comforts, as Robinson Crusoe was able to do. There was a cliff, with eggs on it, and the sea and the sky. We hear of people who escape from prisons by building tunnels with their bare hands, but he could not bore his way through the centre of the earth. What superiority this man possessed he had to use against himself, against his outraged instincts, against the fury of his underfed appetites, against the luciferous revolt of his ego and the awareness of his frustration. There was no other solution for the man but to accept, with an immense detour of the imagination, his plight, and to rebuild his outlook on life around the few elemental facts which had become its sole content.

We are permitted to surmise that he found his peace, though the fever of the old Adam seems not to have burnt itself out. The account of the slates is not tinged by the temper of triumph but of resignation. Yet it ends, for Chamisso was a Kantian, with the realization that the victim of Salas y Gomez, though certainly robbed of many tangible facts which normal life among the multitude would have given him, nevertheless was always in the presence of two intangible facts, two great mysteries, the contemplation of which was not prevented by his cruel confinement: the stars above and God in his heart. The stars wrote in golden hieroglyphs over the canopy of night an allegory of his physical insignificance. With no companion other than astronomical distances, his own dwarfish dimensions must have seemed to him ludicrous. Before this tribunal of immensity his complaints caused no echo. His situation was like that of a mosquito starting to argue about the deficiencies of its biological outfit.

Yet there was the god in his heart. Immensities were the proper food for this god. As a matter of fact the god could develop better on Salas y Gomez than in Paris or London. Because of him, the great dance of the fiery orbs was not lost. As the years passed, a kind of mystic marriage between the heavenly chorus and the two-legged worm on his pillory took place. It was the god who forced the luckless voyager to contribute to the harmony of the Universe by outgrowing the pangs of his dwarfish physique. The inexorable repetition of day and night, which for years tortured him like a succession of boiling hot and ice-cold baths, ended by fanning his imagination into an unsuspected kind of magnificence; he incorporated in his system shooting stars, and the dolphins which played in the evening sun; even the birds which fed him, and which he loathed because of their noisy self-assertion caricaturing the paroxysm of his own self-assertion, rounded out inspiringly his gestures with their elegant gyrations.

Thus the man without a country became a man of all countries. On the lonely altar polished by the great winds of the Pacific he had been forced to sacrifice his human inheritance; with all his curses, all the subtle self-immolation of the spirit, all his piercing cries of protest he could not restore his former status. Destiny forced him to look for his status in a viewpoint which was served not by his own eyes but by the eyes of the Absolute. To gain the ultimate freedom of consent he had to walk through twenty or thirty years of unredeemed thinking. To be sure, there are anchorites who voluntarily retire into graceless regions with not a spot to be thankful for, and who do violence to their human inclinations as veritable gladiators of the soul before an unmoved gallery of coyotes and desert foxes; but this is a profession they have chosen themselves.

We, I mean the citizens of this twentieth century, are rather in the position of the man of Salas y Gomez than of professional anchorites. If we could help it we would never choose exalted views. The whole history of our time is a defense against the necessity of seeing the human situation in a com-prehensive perspective. One hesitates to say that which is repeated so often by professional theologians, but it should be said naturally, spontaneously, without any indignation or pedagogical intent, as if it were a statement about temperature or the definition of a physical law. The struggle of the nineteenth century and of the middle class to stop the bottomless pit of the Universe with a kind of fanatical self-sufficiency, and what has been called an atrophy of the emotions, was a brave one. It has yielded enormous results, baffling in their magnitude; it was a crusade like any other, a growth like any other, with pride as its nucleus; it was a dazzling experiment in short-range philosophies, a paradoxical shortcut to happiness by the roundabout way of capitalistic production; it was originally a reaction against the tediousness of scholasticism and against a meekness in the face of want for which the temper of the Renaissance was unsuited. But the thrilling repudiation of spiritual and unprofitable issues by occidental man was not the last word, just as the man on Salas y Gomez did not end by counting the things he had lost, and by measuring his earthly lot with the yardstick of society.

Like the unhappy-happy adventurer on his Pacific rock, we are asked to part with many things. The flamboyant causes which warmed the hearts of our fathers are no longer ours. Even the second world war was more than anything else a struggle for survival—to put it bluntly, a survival in the face of nothingness, as on Salas y Gomez. Even the Nazis, with the exception of a few particularly paranoiac types, knew that the one thing they professed to be sure of, their hatred, was a fake. It is impossible to say yes without saying no, or at least without knowing that there is a "no." When all is said and done, the drama of our time is a vain interruption of a vacuum. So many façades of meaning are professing to screen meaninglessness that one is tired and falls back on bare techniques and lets it go at that. It doesn't matter whether the techniques are employed in a plus or minus sense; the main point is that they work. And these many techniques in peace and war, techniques of organizing markets and extracting teeth, and building tanks and shooting guns, are kept in an ever accelerated motion by one thing only: the precarious problem of keeping alive. The will to live, described in ponderous terms by the pessimist Schopenhauer, is migrating from the positive to the negative pole of our society. To brave the overwhelming emptiness of the Universe by continuing and expanding the business of reproduction is exposed as a purposeless biological atavism. The empires of our grandparents needed an increasing birthrate in order to boost tribal glories; we know better, and incapable of arresting the mania of being alive, we are content with regulating the traffic without illusions.

In all the nakedness of a shipwrecked sailor, mankind is clinging to its dancing atom, the tumbling rock chained by a magnetic string to a ball of fire. The pressure of events is such that mankind resents being called anything but naked. It has lost its clothes and flaunts its poverty in the face of heaven, choosing, in a kind of protesting mood, to be inexorably sincere about it. This is particularly the preoccupation of materialists and cynics who, if words could kill, would gladly prepare this ruined star for the final descent of the stratospherical deathbreeze; while fascists, officially motivated by a zeal to rescue shattered myths, actually exterminate mankind for the sake of a theory which again amounts to nothing else but biology at its most vicious. Regarded from this angle, life is matter, a digestive machine polluting the air for a few years or decades with its breath, slime in ferment, a kind of self-perpetuating dirt. Matter is an aberration of the great void; therefore the liquidation of living matter is as meaningless as its creation or its maintenance, and might be even more meritorious in view of a quick restoration of the initial nothingness.

"To aim lower than God is in a Christian civilization the first cause of all disorder," writes Jacques Maritain.[1] This would be true even if there were no God, a question we are not to decide. Because society is ruined by the bad habit of taking ecstasies and catastrophes of the physique, sexual and martial, for the only reality, we are forced into the good habit of assuming that there is a God, and of living up to this assumption. This is not meant in the Voltairean sense that if there were no God he ought to be invented, that is, as a social expedient; but in the sense that our constitution is actually harbouring a source of inspiration which cannot flow without previous good habits of thinking and feeling.[2] The habit of thinking and feeling in terms of secular rewards only makes Caliban grin at his own ugliness.

"La France s'ennuie," cried the pampered subjects of Louis Philippe, and raised the more exciting Louis Napoleon upon the throne, the sad-eyed forerunner of the dictators of our times. Our lonely inhabitant of Salas y Gomez, without any opportunity to electrify his days by picking a dictator as his guide, or indulging in less harmful pastimes, must have found his only consolation in the thought of self-destruction in a kind of private total war; until it dawned upon him that the very absence of gadgets by which his time could be whittled down was his great chance. The stars above and God in his heart! Whether this lofty concept was a myth or not, in adjusting his consciousness to it he discovered at last something to live for after the body, deprived of its usual intoxications, had failed miserably to hand him a passport for the continuation of his journey.

From now on the object of his life was the building up, stone by stone, of his consciousness. This beautiful spiritual architecture penetrated his whole being, changed the complexion of his dreams, organized the amorphous mass of his waking hours, and slowly lifted him into the regions where the myriad contradictory impulses which keep the Universe in motion converge. I repeat: We do not know whether it was a myth by which he was integrated, but we know that he was endowed with a faculty to change his experiences into an idea, and to change the macrocosm by which he was surrounded—ocean, sky, sun, and stars—into an idea, and to join these two ideas, and to feel one with the *summum bonum* from which this wealth of relations seemed to proceed. Not to have used this faculty would have killed him.

For not having used this faculty the capitals of Europe are Sodoms and Gomorrhas, consumed by the fire with which they have played from too close a distance. This opinion is held today by prophets and would-be prophets who thirty years ago filled their pages with the thunder of the machine age and denounced savagely any romantic and otherworldly notions which tended to check secular efficiency. Thirty years ago Spengler conceived his formidable barrack of steel, concrete, and asphalt; while now a hardy sociologist from Harvard like Mr. Sorokin[3] employs his grim vocabulary to predict the end of relative—or human—truths, and a new approach to the absolute.

In Sodom and Gomorrha the flesh was in its own; its satisfaction was perfectly organized; the houris and vices travelled from afar in pomp, bought by the gold which delirious slaves with bloodshot eyes extracted from sterile ground. The laboratories of carnal delight were busy creating effects which sent the body through the gamut of sensations while the imagination died before the closed gates of creative time. Obviously the cursed biblical metropoles are the neighbours of our own ostentation; and if the rain of fire is our own invention, nevertheless an offended spirit makes us use our wits against ourselves.

Suddenly there is a change. Revolutions and wars are no longer rhythmic, inescapable, seasonable eruptions by which the energies of society are climaxed and celebrated; they become frightful symptoms which are read through the glasses of a changing consciousness. We are forced to rethink our inherited symbols in the light of a consciousness which starts, like that of the shipwrecked man in the Pacific, on bare rock face to face with the unveiled infinities of time and space. The sequence of our disasters is interrupted by a kind of unexpected metaphysical caesura.

Our thesis is that the frantic insistence on immediate success which gave the nineteenth century such an unholy push toward the quantitative side prepared merely the realization of man's smallness in the frame of quantity. Hitler is a caricature of the type of man so much in view in what was and is and will be for a long time nineteenth century, I mean the man who derives prestige from a performance in unrelated efficiency. One could have pointed out, and I suppose one did, that the whole phenomenon of Hitler is, in spite or because of the supermodern methods of organization he used, a reactionary phenomenon—a piece of Renaissance washed on the shores of the twentieth century, which is no longer Renaissance but which suffers from the Renaissance tradition of man's sole glory as from a mortal germ. It is the protest of forgotten man who has not yet had his day of glory against the impending abdication of man. We are the witnesses of a revaluation of man's place in the Universe.

We have to say a few more things about the man on Salas y Gomez, were it only because this Crusoe *in extremis* would seem at first sight to deny destiny any chances to find fulfillment through a human entelechy. He had to learn his lesson slowly by peopling his solitude with the rhythm of night and day until his very movements, as he circled and scaled the cliff, revealed that he was no longer lonely but was aided by the dance of myriad friendly atoms. At last his imagination was able to grasp that alone though he was, basically he was not alone. He had as companions his growth, the operations of his body, its sicknesses and miraculous recuperations, his flashes of insight—flashes which were prepared in the great cradle of night without his asking. The ever-expanding orchestra of his sensibility was his companion, and so was the mounting sympathy of the cosmos. He had as ally also his dejections and his decay. Without these monsters gaining dominion over him he would not have had cause to reach into the depths for the panacea of a creative impulse. Whole provinces of his being would have been left unvisited.

He had as ally his exercises, bodily and spiritual, by which he helped and facilitated his integration. He made of breathing an art. God's breath which had animated the clay rolled through his body like tides irrigating a desert, received by his organism as the sail receives the wind, and the globe its precarious balance. He was visited by breath as Abraham was visited by the angels.

He had no choice but making the Whole his specialty. Sometimes he was enamoured with nothing but the bitterness in his heart and he felt like a Prometheus chained to his Pacific Caucasus who welcomed the eagle that tortured him because the torture strengthened his case against God—the terrible *j'accuse* of the fallen angel. And yet, against expectations and almost against his wish, the Whole, by the sheer splendor of its organization, engulfed his rebellious ego. The drama of the Universe, a caravan of myriad torches through the night, called for a spectator, for a mind free enough, nay, empty enough in the mystic sense, to comprehend it. According to old fables diamonds have been found in the heads of dragons. The love of the Demiurge is really his willingness to grow a diamond, the spirit, in the heads of small forsaken men and to shape this jewel until he recognizes a ray of his true intentions in it as in a mirror.

First, there was the physical Universe. The man on Salas y Gomez accepted it. The ocean was a fact, so was the blind stone which was his foothold, the fleeting reflection of the waves, the smells of seaweed and fish, the salty taste in his mouth, the limitations of his body which was the victim of a strategy of facts, the prisoner of a conspiracy of facts.

But there was also the spirit—a fact too, but not imprisoned by physical law. While there were many facts in Nature, the essence of the spirit—which made itself felt only belatedly as we have seen—was One. He was born with the diamond in his head, it grew with him, and because his situation did not allow any compromises, any conventional detours and alleviations, it mirrored, that is it "lived," existence in its Oneness. His spirit was disciplined not by proprieties and usages, or by the ordinary hazards of competition, but by an enormous tête-à-tête with the principle of being. "God has no style: His idiosyncrasy is Being." [4] One might paraphrase this: "His idiosyncrasy is Oneness." Every separate thing in the world eventually enters the scales of unity.

Once the forgotten man had thoroughly understood that he lived on the very threshold of Being, which was everywhere the same though in different degrees of intensity—no, which was everywhere the same so far as it was spirit, idea, thought, because "deep corresponds to deep"—once he had thoroughly understood that he could not escape Being, the Oneness of Being, as "earth cannot escape the sky," he could, like Midas, touch everything and it became gold.

A man who walks to the ocean and touches water touches all water. A thing of beauty once understood essentially, not subjectively, is the whole realm of beauty understood. Schopenhauer wrote that the Universe is congealed music; a ray coming from a great musician is enough to make it liquid and fluent again. The petrified facts, the hidden and dull laws, the inexorable causality of the physical Universe dissolved into Being, into a medium by which a divine thought was expressed, always the same thought and always the same language however multiform the expression. It was Being, and its infinite correspondences, which gripped the lonely man and made his imagination as busy as a beehive. Or was it he himself who started this meaningful commotion? To ask this makes us accomplices, distasteful in the eyes of Mr. Maritain, of Kant's "subjectivist poison" and of the German idea of *Einfuehlung*.⁵ The man on Salas y Gomez knew nothing about such intellectual tours de force. Incessantly he wandered over the steps of his physical existence, through the alarms of his senses, toward the limit where the Primum Mobile began, that is the thought, the dream, the effusion which was so rich it needed a Universe to illustrate its power adequately.

Because he acquired the habit, the regal and grandiose habit, of starting the contemplation of his small and yet so infinite world not within himself, but at the threshold of the miraculous centre dominating the body of facts by which he was surrounded and which worked in his own organism as well as in the great One, he could no longer dissociate his living, thinking, and feeling from the Arch Being which constantly crystallized in him and around him. He too began to think mountains, seas, climates, nations, tyrannies and liberties, loves and enmities; he began to think them not as an individual but as one with the Logos, which built up its life in time. "If reality is creation," says Bergson, "it is in our creative moments that we seize reality." Our moments are creative when they do not cater to our own individual ends but to the thoroughly mysterious ends of the Whole—which, humanly speaking, are perhaps not ends at all. "God made all things through me when I had my existence in the unfathomable ground of God." This is Master Eckhart, the oracle of the Middle Ages.⁶

When our man walked over the shore, the rhythm of his steps was not his rhythm but the rhythm of the god who walked in him and through him. Therefore the rhythm did not end with him; it extended infinitely. As he walked rhythmically like a god, and in intimate conjunction with a god, over the poor shore which was building and rebuilding its mineral and animal matter under the impact of storms and torrents of sunshine, he did not enter his personal rhythm but all the potentialities of rhythm in past and future, a huge orchestra of rhythm whose fullness he was able to live while the Logos was able to create it by thinking it. Merely by walking he connected himself with the motion by which the eternal Logos saw fit to expand into time—a motion total in its particularity, the ocean expressed by the waves. Walking conjured up the coming and going of aeons, and the aeon, as the Greeks said, is a child playing dice and jesting.

Because our man walked in consonance with heaven, he perceived all the consequences of this heavenly walking. The Arch Being, in the fullness of its motion, rose thunderously to its height in the consciousness of the lost little man. The Arch Being needed all the migrations, the seasons of the year, of man and of history, all the vibrations of leaves in the forests and of waves and of light, all the meetings and partings, the endless enactment and re-enactment of the earthly and celestial scene, to express properly the scope of his enormous dream, or his enormous walking—which is the same, or one. The Arch Being really did not need all this, but it saw fit to illustrate its riches with an image of infinite complexity. The effort by which this illustration was built up would be wasted if there were not brought into activity a consciousness somewhere which, by combining the parts of the gigantic paradigm, was able to detect the meaning of it, the original text which the illustration was trying to serve. The little lost man was given the key to the mystery, and by using it incurred the gratitude of heaven. To be discovered in the consciousness of man is the interest heaven earns from the capital it has invested in creation. The man on Salas y Gomez, having attempted unsuccessfully for twenty or thirty years to stop the arch-dreamer from dreaming in him, and the arch-walker from walking in him, at last connected his own imagination, for better and for worse, with the imagination of heaven. *Fata volentem ducunt, nolentem trahunt.*[7]

I read once of a modern "initiate": "If she took up a handful of sand from the steppe she saw the oceans of vanished epochs, submarine flora, fantastic animals." [8] Ambroise Vollard tells us that Manet exclaimed when he saw in Venice juicy Brenta gourds in a heap: "Beturbaned heads of Turks! Trophies from the victories of Lepanto, of Corfu!" This I do not mention in praise of phantasmagorias, but in order to show that there are sunsets and victories in a handful of dust and in gourds. Jesus drew wisdom from a mustard seed. Nothing fails to put on holiday garb when the bridegroom comes, an illuminated consciousness.

"What, when the sun rises do you not see a round disk of fire something like a guinea? Oh, no, no," cries Blake. "I see an innumerable company of the heavenly host crying: Holy, holy, holy is the Lord God Almighty." Shakespeare, Rimbaud, looking into an eye or into a river, saw suddenly the ages on which matter dances like the golden ball on the top of the fountain. Alchemy, says Baader, a German romanticist, is the art of distilling the divine substance from the earthly substance. By practising this alchemy the outcast in the Pacific became the centre of the world; his dismal pedestal became a New Helicon washed by all the waters of Grace. By reading the dreary objects of his physical existence—like a pianist reading the insignificant dots and lines of the musical score—as hints and symbols related to an epic idea floating with its train of constellations through infinity, his consciousness, so dejected, so abandoned, so crushed when measured with a human yardstick, was permitted to wander in glory in the footsteps of Being.

Swedenborg, who like Baudelaire after him, wrote profoundly if cryptically about correspondences between the natural and spiritual world, maintains that to ancient peoples the knowledge of correspondences was the chief of knowledges, that they therefore conversed with angels and that natural things served them as a kind of lightning rod for the influx of heaven. This is no plea on behalf of Swedenborgianism. The only thing we are concerned with is the fact, the possible fact, that the man on Salas y Gomez changed the absolute nihilism of his situation through the acquisition of a creative habit into the most brilliant experience open to human consciousness. He unlocked the "seminary of first things." There was nothing in his surroundings which was not "first thing." The island on which he was imprisoned was the sketch of a continent: its very barrenness provoked Being to remodel it and complete it in another million years, and the human imagination which was married to Being sailed ahead, charting the ocean of potentiality. By thus functioning as an *avantgarde* of heaven the imagination of our shipwrecked adventurer animated also that which was mortal in him; it put a light and a fire into the house of clay, just as certain ascetics in the Himalayas protect their bodies in a waste of ice and snow with the heat which their spirit engenders.[9]

We have chosen the example of the man on Salas y Gomez because spirit, like electricity, cannot be defined, but its effects, as in the case of electricity, can be demonstrated. The Kantian Chamisso made of his hero the parade grounds for the enormous manoeuvres of the stars above and the moral law, or God, in his heart. It was the only chance the forsaken man had: either to live the greater life, the macrocosm, which loyally followed him into his exile, or to insist on his small life and to perish. It is our contention that society in general is sufficiently exiled, sufficiently dehumanized, sufficiently severed from inherited human attachments, to make it imperative for society either to eat the bread of the macrocosm or to perish in the attempt to recover its attachments in the wrong, or literal, way. For society, having utilized every shred of energy in physical nature, having tapped the stores of power accumulated by an endless procession of time on earth, having shifted its own constitution from one extreme to the other for the sake of efficiency, and having even changed the symbolic content of its attachments into mere generators of efficiency, cannot, for plain reasons of expediency, do otherwise but crown the giant body it has created with a head that looks through the nature of society's million fetishes to the nature of things, the ultimate One.

Our contemporary society, exiled into the ice age in which the pastures of human idyls are requisitioned by the science of collective survival, is bound to hear, behind the noise of its moves and countermoves which change the physical nature of things, the promise of a new conception of the world based on the nature of things as a Whole. There are limits to physical changes in space, but there are no limits to understanding man's achievements in space from the point of view of the Ultimate, which is not affected by these achievements. If the Ultimate is not affected, we are not affected either, because the mythic original behind our superficial conceits *is* the Ultimate. Basically we are affected only in so far as we realize that in changing things, in achieving things, it is not the result that counts but the operation: the fact that we operate as the man on Salas y Gomez walked, "grandly related" as Thoreau would say, with no other goal but his relatedness.

The globe is no longer expanding. No new continents, no new Americas will arise to offer mankind a fresh start. But while the emergence of America during the Renaissance signified the emergence of a continent of the will, of human will, the absence of new continents will force us from now on to settle in the continent of connected being and seeing. Not we but our consciousness wanders from result to function. And then if we wander, or function, it is still not we; we wander, or function, as has been said of Shakespeare, allegorically, being satisfied to represent, between two eternities of darkness, the principle of operation as it flares up during its passage through mortality, just like a shooting star during its passage through terrestrial atmosphere.

Goethe speaks in his *Winckelmann*[10] of the prodigality of suns, planets, and moons, of stars and galaxies, of comets and nebulas, of worlds created and in the process of creation, and relates this stupendous effort to the *joie de vivre* of an integrated human being. "When man's fully developed nature operates in the full, when he unites with the world as with a large, beautiful, noble and worthy whole, when the concord of his being carries him into a pure and unfettered elation, then the Universe, if it could become conscious of its feelings, would shout with joy at having arrived at its goal, and admire the summit of its own essence and evolution."

Let us assume the coming peace will have as its aim to provide the Universe with opportunities to "shout with joy"—at least we would insure the benevolent partnership of the cosmos in our peace plans. And the incalculable benefits to be derived from such a partnership might eventually induce us to treat the phychological resources of mankind with at least as much ingenuity or patience as we treat our material resources.

*CHAPTER 1*

# THE MIDDLE CLASS AND EUROPE

> *Few middle class ideas, materialistic and utilitarian, are vital in the German mind. It is futile to use them in appealing to Germany because the German mind has rejected them consistently.*
>
> —Dorothy Thompson

STENDHAL, WHO LIVED FAR INTO THE GILDED MEDIOCRITY of Louis Philippe's reign, was one of the first to honor crime as what it has become to thousands of movie directors since: a source of pristine energy in a colorless society. The criminal, sailing on the wave of his passion or in the clutches of his obsession to some inferno of his own making before the eyes of smug and pedestrian contemporaries, has earned the gratitude of genius, who is an outcast himself. Daumier, in cartoons which vibrate with sarcasm at the expense of plutocrats, attacks not the enemy but the defender of society. His judges and lawyers are vulture-like creatures marked with the stupidity of their prejudices and ambitions, who send the creative element of the people to the gallows. William Blake talks darkly of the way of death which is the predatory exertion of the self after innocence has been passed; Virginia Woolf tells us that when a tramp stole Roger Fry's watch, the latter's comment was, "Mais comme ces gens sont moralement supérieurs aux bourgeois." [1]

The criminal, in the course of the nineteenth and twentieth centuries, becomes the voice of nature, the theme of countless psychological romances, the acrobat of life in a world which lacks the courage to escape the evil eye of drudgery by asocial acts. As we might have expected, Fascism and Nazism did not fail to be heralded in a literature of great brilliance and effectiveness, which teases and scares the bourgeois with the stage thunder of immoralism. Mario Praz, who in his book *Romantic Agony* [2] has collected in a blasé but learned manner countless instances of literary sadism, lumps together Swinburne, Barrès, and d'Annunzio as types who spiced their schemes with the awful energies that grow outside the well-groomed playgrounds of the bourgeois. So far as Germany is concerned, we shall meet the solitary Nietzsche frequently in the course of this essay. "The criminal type," he wrote, almost in the words of his beloved Stendhal, "is the type of the strong man under unfavourable conditions—the strong man who has been made sick." The most talented literary pioneer of Nazism, Ernst Juenger, wrote in *Der Arbeiter*, with regard to the bourgeois and his attempts to guide the German destiny after 1918: "Here ends every discussion, here we can do nothing but assume a silence that gives us a premonition of the silence of death. Here the German youth had no choice but to proclaim its adherence to a rebellion which left no doubt whatever that

## THE MIDDLE CLASS AND EUROPE    21

in this context it is infinitely more desirable to be a criminal than to be a bourgeois." [3]

There is good reason to ponder the equivocal position the middle class occupies in the imagination of continental Europe. In spite of many splendid analyses of the European temper, the collapse outside Anglo-Saxon countries of the ideologies and institutions derived from the French Revolution remains an enigma to those who overlook the peculiar psychological problems provoked by middle-class rule. This rule one might call light and enlightened. As a matter of fact, it was supposed to be almost no rule at all; a set of ideas and institutions called liberalism was engaged to remove rule from the path of mankind. And yet, apparently by its very lack of guidance, it proved in the long run exceedingly unsatisfactory. Everybody is acquainted with the unexpected turn for the worse, to put it mildly, which economics took in a world that had lost confidence in laissez-faire philosophy, a world that was illogically patching up the holes in the system with high tariffs and government subsidies. But the psychological basis for discontent with the middle-class way of doing things in Europe is not so obvious to Anglo-Saxons. It is occasionally stated that "laissez faire is a philosophy of the economically strong, not of the economically weak." This is acknowledged even in conservative economic textbooks. Yet in every other sphere, and particularly in a psychological respect, the advantages of liberalism seem so enormous that the dangerous gyrations and insecurities of the business cycle seem not too high a price for the preservation of the liberal way of life.

There is a psychological aspect of middle-class unpopularity in Europe, and though scientists have refrained from stressing it, it deserves popularization—especially in view of possible attempts at "re-education" of rebellious European nations, Germany in particular. Germany has been the hotbed of two world-shaking conspiracies against middle-class standards of respectability, Marxism and Hitlerism; and I submit that nothing is more dangerous than to begin its re-education with the statement that once again the bourgeois has been victorious. It would be much more to the point to say that it was the middle class which failed, or rather the absurd caricature, the ludicrous superlative of petty bourgeois success-philosophy in whose embrace Hitler's anti-middle-class revolution expired. We are not going into that here. Here we are simply concerned with the statement that freedom, a sublime notion, has been embodied and fulfilled by the European bourgeois so unconvincingly, so defectively, that even if he had been able to prevent the Great Depression, yet, for purely psychological reasons, some kind of secession from freedom was due.

I recognize two main elements in the entangled, unholy truculence of Hitler's Germany. One of the components, the one for which Hitler's personal provincialism is responsible—his own special jumble of class and race war—we shall pass over for the time being. But the other component is more than just sheepish response to Hitler's antediluvian hysteria; it is an incident in the general consternation of modern man and needs to be analyzed here. For this purpose it is unfortunately indispensable to consider the ambiguous and abused term "bourgeois." It is a word-fetish commanding the most contradictory reactions, a magic potion taken from the shelf by the political druggist in order to expose his clients to mental and emotional compounds as irreconcilable as water and oil. In one frame of reference the bourgeois is security, respectability, a passport for success, the pillar of achievement, the goal of society; in another he is the predatory monster not only of Blake and the romanticists but also of Marx and the socialists, he is the Jew of the Nazis and the Aryan of the Asiatics, the paragon of insipidity in the eyes of philosophers and an object of melancholy ridicule to the inhabitants of Greenwich Village and the Quartier Latin.

It is clear that the different evaluation is considerably influenced by whether you stand in the ranks of the bourgeoisie

## THE MIDDLE CLASS AND EUROPE 23

or in the ranks of the impecunious majority which resents the fact that it is not of the bourgeoisie. But apart from this well-known panorama of the class struggle the bourgeois is a mighty scarecrow that is alternately torn to pieces and patched up in a battle royal among many ideological birds. The confusion is immense, and the most tragic part of it is that people no longer know whether the bell tolls for freedom or for the bourgeoisie.

There is a particular reason why people are loath to enter upon a frank discussion of this dubious issue. America, for the second time in a quarter of a century, strains every nerve to preserve freedom on this globe. She deserves the undying gratitude of anybody who watches with a new hope the legions of brotherhood descend into the last nook and corner of our planet and dispel the spook of organized brutality. Yet the stormwind composed of power and gentleness, which blows from the New World over the old continents in order to thaw the winter of ideologies, blows from a country which is unmistakably harbouring the bourgeois. As a matter of fact, a certain poll has allegedly ascertained that eighty per cent of the American people pride themselves on being thought of as members of the middle class. Here the matter stands, so far as America is concerned, and there could be nothing more natural and desirable. But in the view of continental Europe there is no real comfort connected with a philosophy which climaxes in a bourgeois. The evaluation of the term "bourgeois" is not only dependent on the class from which you look at the matter, but on the region too. There is a huge gulf in this respect between Europe and America. But to speak about it is difficult, if not preposterous, if you have prayed with all your heart for the victory of American arms. To doubt the validity of the bourgeois philosophy has been in general the poisonous practice of freedom's enemies.

The difficulty of asserting that a revolt against the bourgeois is going on in Europe apart from Hitler's revolt, and will continue to go on after Hitler's downfall, would have seemed insuperable to me if I had not happened to come across the *Lettre aux Anglais* by Georges Bernanos.[4] Ordinarily the enunciations of European expatriates who have settled in the Americas during this second world war suffer from an understandable bewilderment, a desire to please their hosts, to help their own causes, to prove practical, effective, to the point. On the whole, not Europeans are speaking, but diplomats of distress, hope, and vengeance, who build up their cases with the confident language of their host. But Mr. Bernanos' pages, written in exile in Brazil by a Catholic Frenchman, are uncompromisingly European.

There is a tortured air in Europe, an uncertainty which grew and grew for a long time, long before Hitler took over and endeared himself to men of bad will by creating certainties of the most obvious kind—the old routine of pressure and counter pressure, offered without the condiment of civilization. Instead of condemning Hitler and praising civilization, which is by all means the proper thing to do, Mr. Bernanos does the unorthodox thing of wondering whether a return to the status quo, when the war of all against all had at least the flavor of civilization about it, is really the last word that can be said on the subject of this monumental crisis. "Cher M. Roosevelt," cries Mr. Bernanos—for the Americans are included in the *Lettre aux Anglais*, "this war will have dishonored the regimes built on force, but it will not have rehabilitated the regimes built on complacency. Once more the peoples will have lost illusions; they will not have found a faith." "Our peoples," he writes a few pages earlier, "do not perhaps know very well what they want; but they do not want a certain conception of life which it is not unjust to call 'bourgeois.' The peoples do not want any longer a camouflaged materialism, a materialism which, in order to define and justify itself, exploits the vocabulary of morality and spirit, with the support of a great number of Christians. They prefer misery and death to the insidious mediocrity which gradually covers our civilization like mildew, to the polytechnical mediocrity, to the horrible nothingness of comfort. The peoples of Europe prefer to perish (Les peuples d'Europe préfèrent crever)."

Mr. Bernanos' book, inhabited by the spectres of Europe, was welcomed in this country because it had the ring of truth. John Jay Chapman once said: "So long as there is any subject which men may not freely discuss, they are timid upon all subjects." The bourgeois is an uncomfortable subject, yet it is welcomed because today we seem to feel that agreeable subjects are not the necessary ones. Bernanos' book was neither correct nor diplomatic, but terribly sincere. Those expatriate Europeans who read it felt that for once the black magic of the totalitarian drive was countered by a kind of white magic, that for once intensity was matched by intensity. It was not that somebody who was struck hit back and then stopped; he hit back yet did not stop but pursued the evil to its source and found it, partially at least, in himself, in the bourgeois, in the correct citizen of the age of progress. The end of the great spiritual battle which had congealed into a dreamy, beloved form called Europe, the smashing of that form, its reduction to pleistocene dust, or rather the dust of the cemetery, is not explained by the removal of such bastions of civilization as law, reason, and prosperity; no, perhaps the civilization that needed these bastions was in itself un-European. What did the age of progress do for the cause of European integration— aside from accelerating train schedules? With what incantations did it lift the European mind over the pitfalls of time, aside from provoking, by its very monstrosity, a few pathetic protests? Did men really turn over night into animals because a peddler in plushy sunsets and cardboard mirages with the name of Hitler walked the highways of Germany? This is the fallacy exposed by Mr. Bernanos.

Mr. Bernanos is a Catholic and it is easy to contend that he had an axe to grind in blaming the anthropocentric civilization of our age for setting the avalanches in motion. What I am trying to do is to support Mr. Bernanos' thesis from a purely worldly angle, with no fixed theology in the background; from the point of view of a man who was born a bourgeois and who discovered, much to his disgust, that to lose one's worldly substance does not mean to cease to be a bourgeois; a man who uses the term bourgeois merely as a "convenient working fiction" to denote that part in modern man that is inflated by the dead strength of our civilization to the point where he is ordering the Universe instead of being ordered by it.

It is clear that "universe" too is a convenient working fiction, like God, as an agnostic would say; it is a fiction that is supposed to stand for an inexpressible reality which, in the long run, makes the expressible reality of the anthropocentric civilization appear like a fiction. If I am occasionally rash and reckless enough to help my argument with a harmony or symbol borrowed from the church, I can say only that it is impossible to believe in the vitality of the spirit and to ignore the vitalization of the Occident through the Christian idea. It is obvious that the European catastrophe and the catastrophe of the Christian idea are related.

The decadence and humiliation of Europe is so crushing, on the other hand, that every historical organization through which the Spirit manifests itself is affected. The spiritual principle as such needs assertion not through hallowed formulas but through spontaneity. In this terrible moment there is no particular edition of this principle that needs defining, but the soul must be born naked again before it can be dressed. Walter Pater once wrote that we should not waste our time with distinctions like classicism and romanticism; the issue really is whether a thing is alive or dead, or, as Matthew Arnold said, whether it is of the party of "Geist" or of "Ungeist."

## THE MIDDLE CLASS AND EUROPE 27

The generation of Europeans which is condemned to witness the disintegration of the Occident has discovered that the forces that atomize and pulverize effectively have not the power to console. This generation is obsessed by the idea that their ancestors, before they became bourgeois, had reservoirs of meaning at their disposal, and that the evaporation of these reservoirs preceded the evaporation of the continent that was theirs. As far back as I can remember, my generation in Europe has blamed the bourgeois for having emptied the reservoirs of meaning, for having torn the style of the continent to pieces, for having made adjustment to physical environment the pedestal of self-glorification and for having made the inner environment a joke, for having buried the tension between fact and symbol, for having turned the dance of the world genius into a marathon of personal success. These are romantic notions. It seems that Don Quixote cannot die.

The status of the bourgeois in America is quite different. The bourgeois is a European invention. I once saw in the jungle of Cambodia, in Angkor, an American, inventor of a contraption which has a smoothing influence on our physique in connection with shaving operations, riding on a palanquin through the balmy moonlight, exactly like the plutocrat in Booth Tarkington's novel; the sleepy Cambodians and the almond-eyed Cambodiennes were electrified by his presence, a circumstance no doubt aided by the way he scattered a generous portion of his fortune from his wavering throne amongst the scrambling natives. No European capitalist will ever attain such poetical heights. The gestures of a European are ever frustrated by his watchfulness and circumspection; or, if he tries to assume Caesarean unconcern in a vain manoeuvre against old-age inhibitions, the horror before his own boldness thaws the snowbridge of his assurance. The ostentation of the European bourgeois is stolen, and therefore rouses no enthusiasm; in the ostentation of the American in Cambodia, Life itself, being its own stage director, celebrated its invincible freshness. The American capitalist is classless—grandee, entrepreneur, and proletarian all in one—while the European capitalist is ever nursing the wounds he brings home from conflict with the classes above and below him.

Nietzsche apostrophizes the bourgeois in *Human, All Too Human:* "You rich bourgeois... the spurious histrionic element in your pleasures, which lie more in the feeling of contrast (because others have them not, and feel envious) than in feelings of realized and heightened power—these are the things that spread the poison of that national disease, which seizes the masses ever more and more as a Socialist heart-itch, but has its origin and breeding place in you." Nietzsche identifies socialism with resentment. The European who comes to America is more impressed by the absence of resentment than by skyscrapers.

The different evaluation of the middle class in Europe and in America means a different evaluation of the crisis which turns our civilization against itself; it means a different evaluation of the French Revolution and its consequences which led mankind from a corrupt Olympus to a glorified hell. Though America is tunnelled and mined by Indian echoes which occasionally burst into the open as colors on Mexican murals, the American soil was nevertheless free from associations so far as the makers of the nineteenth century were concerned; they lived in the present, and only fastidious souls cared for what Van Wyck Brooks calls the "garlanding" of the virgin continent "with associations." This job was not done by literati and historians—though they contributed—but by the actions of the railroad age, by people who were alive. In Europe it had been done already by the dead.

This great melodious death which makes Europe a *pompe funèbre* of spent loves was absent in America. Death was too melodious in Europe; it was the sad prodigy which stopped the living with hints of faded glory. It made one wish that the living, before they floated the schemes which dazzled by sheer intensity in America, would undergo a second birth first, like the Brahmins, because everything they did and could do was entirely out of place.

Commercialism, because of the competition of the illustrious dead and the dreams the dead had dreamt, was always something of a heresy in Europe, the dawn of prose after the sunset of poetry. In America, on the contrary, the advent of trade and its apotheosis in an unprecedented crescendo of activity was rushing into a wilderness which had waited for aeons to be raped. These interminable abandoned woods, beloved by Chateaubriand and Thoreau, were satiated with aimless growth, and longed to expire in the arms of an organizing will. While commercialism in Europe was the end of a style, in America it was the beginning of rational selective processes. The majestic solitudes were put under the yoke of a discipline which in itself was a victory over man's sluggish propensities. The trade empire that emerged had, compared to the absence of system in Nature and the happy-go-lucky ways of the Indian, an ascetic element; it was charmless method eclipsing the irresponsibility of lotos eaters. The enormous task of filling the mountains and plains of America with the inexorable rhythm of duty—duty, says Goethe, is the day's postulate —received a kind of semi-religious sanction; it was repetition, in a protestant temperature, of the *Gesta Dei per Francos*, with the three dimensions to be conquered instead of the infidels.

The bourgeois in nineteenth-century America, who was a dynamic man, was also a rebel. He was originally a rebel against the indulgences of the flesh, a dissenter, a puritan; he rebelled against an order that filled Europe with falsehood, so it seemed, and against a primitive and infantile deification of the creature instead of the creator. He stood for purity of the Law and the Word. These were the beginnings only; but to this day nobody has seen America who has not looked behind the stupendous façades of the metropoles and discovered the innumerable tiny white houses which cover the plains under an intense sky and take pride in being inconspicuous, each like virtue's waiting room. The bourgeois disciplined himself in opposition to the feudal fireworks of Europe; he was a conscious advance from dissipation to concentration. "Somewhere deep in every American heart lies a rebellion against the old parenthood of Europe." [5]

No wonder he became the model of a new society, the king of a more rational present—everyone a king in his own right. He commanded respect, while in Europe the bourgeois all through his reign was plagued with the most vicious inferiority complex. In America his mode of life, stripped of the excrescences of uncontrolled fancy which had choked the centuries of "fanaticism," appeared rational and constructive, the only possible way of mastering the restlessly growing century. Science, machine, and money asked for a new kind of strategy which only the bourgeois could provide. In Europe the quaint traditional hierarchy went on borrowing its lustre from extinct volcanoes, but it failed miserably when it became imperative to know how to handle quantities. The over-subtle approaches to life were exploded by the irrepressible forces of a machine age which demanded men without illusions, hard-working, attached to facts—the bourgeois.

The rebellious mood of the puritan passed, but as America sailed ahead and left Europe, frozen in ancient spells, behind, the modern temper remained rebellious. Modernism was the hothouse of undreamed-of potentialities; the catacombs of stuffiness cracked, and all the world outside America became a greenhorn in the art of living breathlessly. The tycoon—hero of an era in which the panorama of existence was illumined by wheat corners, oil monopolies, and steel combines—anticipated with less noise and more success the "dangerous living" gospel of Mussolini.

The fascination of artificial paradises, dripping with the dew of domesticated auroras, was summed up by the enigmatic billionaire, with his over-specialized mind, divorced from nature, feeding on the songs of figures and the fecundity of investments. He could not help being a rebel with relation to a more organic past. After the defeat of 1918 I have known tellurian Prussian junkers crowding the offices of often questionable jobbers and bankers, frantically clinging to the bandwagon of bourgeois success. Incapable of conceiving of life without power, they turned to the only agency where power was to be had, just as the Kaiser's grandson left Potsdam for the Ford plant in Detroit. However, this was only a panicky move, and very soon the junkers learned that power was no longer in the hands of the bourgeois, at least not in Europe.

Politics is another reason for the positive evaluation of the bourgeois in America. Politics in America was a bear tamed in the school of the bourgeois. The tamer did not always need to make an appearance; he was the awe-inspiring power behind the throne. But in Europe, where the state was always exalted into the neighbourhood of providence, the bourgeois as a statesman had no façade. Bismarck and Cavour, Clemenceau and Lloyd George, were not middle class—neither are Churchill and Stalin—but Bethmann and the men of the Panama affair were. This was in European eyes a disastrous shortcoming. The correctness as well as the scandals of the bourgeois implied that he tackled a patriotic task in the spirit of a specialist, using what he had memorized in school but not daring to evoke from the deep the ghost he feared would crush him. He presided over public affairs as if the fatherland were a shop, or he went to the other extreme and relied on the efficacy of academic concepts which had guided the Athenians or the Romans in the squabbles of antiquity. In both cases he, the hard-headed man of practice, was a theorist, and was out of touch with the wild and erratic moods of highstrung nations.

Wilson, however, was a sublimated bourgeois. He embarked

for Europe with that magnificent lack of inhibition, that apostolic assurance, which the European middle-class idealists never could quite muster in the shadow of their atavisms. In Europe middle-class idealists like Mazzini and Carl Schurz became exiles, or passed their lives in the clouds of a respectable but helpless attitude like the liberal opposition of Bismarck. Their inspiration did not dissolve the density of the historical situation, the stubborn assertiveness of age-old demons in the soul of the introverted common man of the old world, caught in the meshes of loyalties, dependencies, and fears. This is the reason why revolutions in Europe are terrible: they have first to smash through the inward checks of the *Untertan*, the human material which is not an end in itself but a means to an end outside itself.

It is an old story how Wilson's idealism clashed with European atavisms—we are ruled by our dead, said Clemenceau, characteristically. "Man is good!" No bourgeois could dare to say that in Europe without being asked by dishevelled poets and barefoot sectarians, who claim the monopoly for saying such things, how much he was trying to make by it. However Wilson said it, and meant it, and here you have the difference between Europe and America.

"Man is good!" Can a bourgeois afford to have ideals? The identity of the profit urge of an acquisitive society and the ideals on which modern society is founded, a view maliciously advertised in Europe, was mellowed in America by the fact that liberty worked. Narrow profiteering was constantly overruled by the adventure of forming a new type of free man in an enormous space slowly filling with hopeful people. The type after which American society tried to model itself was Lincoln. Lincoln, much more than Wilson, achieved the miracle of investing with a golden glow the soberness that steers the middle course. To "institutionalize the Golden Rule" was the very thing that in Europe degenerated to a term of contempt, the *juste milieu*. In America this miracle was possible only because Lincoln was not a conditioned sociological phenomenon but a wave, a towering wave, in the current of life. He was a man first, and next he was "the great American Demos," and then he was the man who declared, "Labor is prior to and independent of capital. No men living are more worthy to be trusted than those who toil up from poverty." He was the man who addressed the workers of Manchester, who had congratulated him for the abolition of slavery, not as class-conscious proletarians but as "Christians." In this sense, and in many other senses, he transcended the labels of sociologists, he was a product of natural morality rather than of social morality.

"The great hegira from northern and central Europe had been largely motivated by the desire to escape from the over-humanized aspects of those lands," writes Mary Austin in her memorable introduction to *American Rhythm*.[6] In a sense America shatters all the anti-bourgeois notions the disillusioned European brings over the Atlantic. While the bourgeois in Europe signifies the end of meaning, and therefore to an extent the end of life, even American artists and writers who have dragged their prophetic gift through real-estate offices, dry-cleaning establishments, shoe-repair shops, and filling stations, are in the end reconciled and absorbed by the sweeping power of the nude fact: Life.

There seems to be nothing that cannot but enhance life's enormous energies. Europe's subtle despairs become irrelevant. People in America seem to become bourgeois because they want more of life, or they run away from the bourgeois, again because they want more of life—life impersonal, a gift, not a claim. There is this life-worship that unites conformist and non-conformist—"The genius of the Maple, Elm and Oak, The secret hidden in each grain of corn."[7] Whitman, who carried the voice of America to Europe's youth much more effectively than Jefferson, Lincoln, or Wilson, includes the bourgeois in his boundless catalogue of acceptances. This is as it should be, because first comes the torrent of life, its crystallizations come later.

The saving grace of America is its impersonality. While in Europe things tend to look for a resting place in some type or character, in America everything is sheer existence, is understandable and excusable only as existence. Like the triumphal chariot of the Church Militant at the end of the *Purgatorio*, Existence is drawn over the scene of the New World not by man but by the gryphon of vital energy. Professor Brownell in his discussions with Frank Lloyd Wright [8] sings the empire of TVA as Virgil sang the empire of Augustus. TVA, he says, is building more than a dam; it is building a civilization. The civilization Professor Brownell sees is exciting—"strange quests enter the scene; the glisten of unknown fish is seen in the net of existence." It is not a bourgeois civilization, not even man's civilization.

The glorification of the human virtuoso, the measuring of the Universe with the human scale, was the *idée mère* of Greece. The return to a Christian Dionysos, the adoration of the maternal Universe symbolized by the Virgin, launched the spirited vagabondage of the Middle Ages. Then followed the incredibly effective Vanity Fair of naturalism, which started with the Renaissance and is now on the point of closing, in so far as it served as a footstool for man's self-assertion. Today Mr. Brownell solemnly declares: Chicago defeats personality. Like "God-driven medieval Europe, the naturalistic modern world is also beyond human scale." We wonder whether history is at an end: Mr. Brownell speaks only of "social configurations of Power." At the centre of the future, and almost of present society, is not shapely man, nor shapely Venus Anadyomene, but unshapely Power, a visitor from the shores of unseen treasure islands which float between galaxies.

In the following pages I am not speaking of the American bourgeois, about whom I know very little, except that he is attractively dwarfed by the energies he has been unloosing; but about the bourgeois I know, the European bourgeois, the German bourgeois, the bourgeois in myself. The psychology of Europe is upset, and as a cure a long ride in the vast autonomy of creation is recommended, instead of a prison term in man-made moulds. Society has always been an asylum for sick souls, an incubator of maladjustment; and in Europe the prescriptions of the bourgeois era, which kept closed all the windows opening onto the Whole, aggravated the malaise until it got out of hand.

Once upon a time, when government was allied to the Cumean and Delphian Sibyl, and to saints like Bernard of Clairvaux and Catherine of Siena, and to prophetesses like Hildegard of Bingen and Mechthild of Magdeburg, it may have failed—from the point of view of an efficiency expert. But it practised what Maurice Barrès, long after Socrates, called "therapeutics of the soul." Efficiency was by no means unknown in the pre-industrial era—the Arsenal in Venice, described in the twenty-first canto of Dante's *Inferno*, mended and loaded ships after a system that recalls vividly the Ford plant—but society supplied each individual with an Ariadne thread with which to find his way back from the dark labyrinth of human assertiveness to a dimension where the human scale was overruled. Under the bourgeois the road of human assertiveness was made a one-way road, and anybody who was foolish enough to turn back toward the solace of superhuman energies was bound to be run over. The ravages of that European epidemic, named "resentment" after Nietzsche's suggestion, can be defined as man's despair at having as a valid ultimate only himself.

To enumerate symptoms of this epidemic is almost like telling the intellectual history of Europe of the last hundred years. Not long ago I read in an American periodical an article, written by a European, in which mention is made of the surprise American officials must have felt when meeting the French naval officers who piloted the battleship "Richelieu" from North Africa to New York. They met for the first time a "mental pattern which to us Europeans is only too familiar: the snarling contempt, the distorted lucid hatred, closed to fact and reason, prompted by a kind of frightful automatism in finding ever new pretexts for animadversion and derision." [9]

So far we have witnessed in the nineteenth and twentieth centuries the transformation of Europeans into one vast mental proletariat, into what the Germans call *Interessentenhaufen*, pressure groups, without any other coherence than the insatiable and inexhaustible inferiority complex and resentment of the individuals whose aggregates they represent. What happened? No wonder people were bitter since the liberal dogma of the outward equality of man was contradicted by the persistence, and even aggravation, of outward inequality. The dogma of the pre-liberal past, on the other hand, accepted outward inequality, but at least realized, in a symbolic order, the fact of man's inward equality.

What is a symbolic society? Plato, in Book VI of the *Republic*, says, "No state can be happy which is not designed by artists who imitate the heavenly pattern." In a symbolic society the diversity of creation is reconciled with its unity. This is only possible by subordinating our daily task to the "pattern laid up in heaven" of which Plato speaks. A symbolic society is not content merely to express daily tasks, daily worries, the preoccupations of the day; its goal is to express, in Time, the Eternity of creation in its depth, or as the Chinese "philosophy of contentment" would put it, the inner principle of Nature. A symbolic society is symbolic of First Things treated as First Things. The authorities are, as in Plato's *Republic*, guardians of First Things rather than the tools of the blind moment. It is a society whose pride is to generate, uphold, and constantly renew the spells and inward perspectives by which the inequalities of the community are purified and organized "from the point of view of deeper equality." [10]

There is no group or profession which is excluded from placing itself, through an act of genuine self-expression, on the magic carpet on which Diversity serves Unity. "This was ritually the moment of the Despised and Rejected," we read in E. M. Forster's *A Passage to India;* "the God could not issue from his temple until the unclean Sweepers played their tune; they were the spot of filth without which the spirit cannot cohere." Even in the utter detachment of Dante's *Paradiso* we have a social hierarchy based on "Amor Fati," acceptance of their limitations by the enlightened. In the third canto Piccarda answers the question whether she can bear the imperfections of status that have remained with her:

> Brother, our will
> Is, in composure, settled by the power
> Of charity, who makes us will alone
> What we possess, and naught beyond desire.
> Rather it is inherent in this state
> Of blessedness, to keep ourselves within
> The Divine Will, by which our wills with His
> Are one. So that as we, from step to step
> Are placed throughout this kingdom, pleases all,
> Even as our King, who in us plants His Will;
>     And in His Will is our tranquillity:
> It is the mighty ocean, whither tends
> Whatever it creates and Nature makes.

Piccarda's beautiful words are the Magna Charta of a world which is primarily concerned with the "therapeutics of the soul."[11] The utter neglect of such concerns in bourgeois Europe—America attempted a solution through the fusion of the classes into one exuberant type—resulted in demoniac workdays and diabolical Sunday afternoons. A French writer[12] describes a Sunday afternoon under the middle-class reign thus: "Everybody in the hamlet, unemployed for a day, was trying to escape from the ordinary routine; and making little progress, envied wealth as the sovereign power.... They hated everything. ... Homely girls surmised that a thirty franc hat would make them beautiful. ... They blamed the government for not being willing to supply money for expenses, comforts and pleasures in the town, the province and everywhere, without demanding any work at all." The people Bazin describes, who participate in the human comedy without beauty and waste the rich French Sunday by counting their grievances, have been taught to be smart. They are willing to transform the rich pastures of their ancestors into an emotional desert, if this makes those who are presumably happier—the middle class—as unhappy as they are.

Within the frontiers of Europe, "closed" forever, work as a weapon of advancement had a blunt edge. The most effective way for the worker to make himself conspicuous, since he learned to look at life rather in terms of advancement than in terms of perfection, was not the excellence of his accomplishment, but its withdrawal. Europe, for a thousand years, had been trained for quality: now it was trained for strikes. An arsenal of craft, of perfection, of good judgment, of sober contentment and self-rewarding style, stocked and stored by the quiet enthusiasm of a thousand years, went up in flames like the Alexandrian library: no barbarian conqueror committed the sacrilege, but the owners of this priceless heritage were persuaded to exchange the good will, the spiritual benefit, of a work well done, for the dubious benefit which awaited them in their capacity as pawns in the class struggle. Their ancestors had turned the ancient curse of labour into something more like a blessing; the modern labourer forced himself, against his better instinct, to see his work as a curse, in order to have a grievance against those who knew how to turn their work if not into a blessing, into something they considered better than a blessing—profit.

In the first decade of the twentieth century Charles Péguy,[13] who came of peasant stock from the banks of

THE MIDDLE CLASS AND EUROPE    39

the Loire and who was killed in the first world war, cried out, "Today, everyone is a bourgeois."

"How has the most laborious people on earth, and perhaps the only laborious people on earth, perhaps the only people that loved work for work's sake, and for honor, or in a word, just loved to work, been changed into this people of saboteurs? .... It is the bourgeoisie who solicit. It is the bourgeoisie who, turning the workmen into bourgeois, have taught them to solicit. Today in this same insolence and in this brutality, in the sort of incoherence which they bring into their demands, it is very easy to sense the hidden shame of being forced to ask, of having been brought, by the new laws of economic history, to solicit. Oh yes, they ask something of someone, nowadays. They even ask everything of everyone." And: "It cannot be repeated too often: all the evil, all the aberration, all the crime has come from the bourgeoisie. It is the bourgeoisie who began the sabotage and all sabotage took birth in the bourgeoisie. This is because the bourgeoisie began to treat the work of man as a security on the stock exchange. It is because the bourgeosie set about speculating perpetually on the work of man in the stock exchange that the workman too, in imitation, collusion and opposition, and one could almost say by agreement, set about speculating perpetually on his own work. It is because the bourgeoisie began to exert perpetual blackmail over the work of man that we live in this regime of speculation and perpetual blackmail."

Surrounded at every turn by repositories of "work well done," with every stone and field and hill echoing some profound suggestion, the European soul of the machine age refused to take the hint and remained suspended between the poles of complacency and resentment. If you had no reason to imprison yourself in the port of complacency, your success depended on your skill in making the Leviathan of resentment work for you. The social revolutionaries did not attempt, naturally, to lift the problem out of its initial antithetical phase to a plane where the "opposites meet," the plane of the *concordantia* and *coincidentia oppositorum*. Whatever the differences between the architects of the great anti-bourgeois revolts which have rocked Europe in the last hundred years, they were one in their frantic attachment to their resentment.

Let me quote the following unusual but entertaining description of the state of mind of Karl Marx:[14] "Among his innumerable hates were the gods, the Christian religion, his parents, his wife's uncle—'the hound'—his German kinsfolk, his own race—'Ramsgate is full of fleas and Jews'—the Prussian reactionaries, his liberal and Utopian socialist allies, the laboring population—'Lumpenproletariat' or 'riff-raff'—democracy —'parliamentary cretinism'—and of course, the British royal family, 'the English mooncalf and her princely urchins,' as he called them. His self-imposed task he defined as 'the ruthless criticism of every thing that exists.'"

His formidable resentment caused Marx to devise on the shoulders of Hegel an interpretation of history which proved to be political dynamite, but about whose objective content Max Eastman said rather cautiously: "Obviously nobody could persuade himself of these fantastic propositions unless he had some reason to do so other than the desire to understand the world."[15] Another maker of German dynamite, another engineer of the world empire of German resentment, Hitler, was hardly motivated by a desire to understand the world either. On the contrary, his supreme incapacity to understand the world in any profound sense was the magnet which attracted the masses, whose instinctive harmony with the world process had been cruelly disrupted as the nineteenth century advanced. About Mussolini Mr. Borgese writes in *Goliath*,[16] "It is as though a tempest of resentment against the Universe itself were bursting in him."

This reduction of the rich cosmos Europe into a seething sea of resentment would not have taken place if the institu-

THE MIDDLE CLASS AND EUROPE 41

tions, habits, and ambitions of the bourgeoisie had captivated the imagination of the masses in an active, productive, fertile sense, in a sense which was not offensive. But the bourgeosie had nothing to captivate the imagination with, because its desire to understand the world in a profounder sense was just as limited as that of its resentful opponents. The desire to understand the world was turned toward material profits, which, because they were material, were exclusive—while spiritual profits are not. The bourgeoisie understood the world from its own point of view, but in this understanding the quality of a satisfying spiritual experience for everybody was lacking.

With this remark we have arrived at the core of this chapter: We as citizens of our age have parted company with "kairos," time in which memories and visions ripen into organic thought and experience. We are left with time that is quick and full of anxiety, that has room only for complacency and resentment. In a later section of this book we shall hopefully envisage a future when man may feel at home again in a time that is as it ought to be, a breeder of wisdom—even in a civilization built by alarm-clock time. At this point let us remark that a secession from profundity was inevitable because "decomposed time" was needed for immediate success.[17]

Originally the machine was supposed to open the hall of intellectual delights to the toiling multitudes and allow them to partake in the symposium at which imperishable food is offered. But the goal was hardly defined in this way. Every student of economics has heard of the "roundabout way of capitalism." If you care for a continuous and ample supply of a want-satisfying good, you do not approach that good directly, but in a roundabout way, devoting your attention first to making all kinds of implements, intermediate products whose interaction will eventually produce a steady flow of the desired good.

Let us assume that the good the bourgeoisie was interested in was happiness. Happiness we defined, when we related the problematic story of the recluse on Salas y Gomez, as an agreement between oneself and the general Being. The process of achieving this agreement, of tuning the inward orchestra to a bolder and higher key, has been called "growth of meaning."[18] It is possible to see in the attempt of the bourgeoisie to make the world safe for its reign an attempt to make the world safe for "growth of meaning." Paul Tillich[19] stipulates as a premise for happiness, or creative self-fulfillment, that "the freedom to follow the objective demands involved in the nature of one's work" be "unrestrained by heteronomous demands coming from outside," in this context, from want. It is possible to interpret liberalism in a Jeffersonian, or static, sense. It is possible to idealize the industrial and commercial operations of the bourgeoisie as concentration on the arts of becoming in the interest of the arts of being, as harnessing of physical energies in order to feather, through elimination of menial tasks, the metaphysical nest.

This could be the inner meaning of the machine age. Such an assumption, however, would imply a willingness on the part of the bourgeoisie to abdicate when control over physical nature is perfected. In reality the roundabout way by which the problem of a meaningful happiness has been approached by the bourgeoisie has become autonomous, a law unto itself. The "desire to understand the world" is there, at least as far as this involves understanding the organization of the physical world. So far as the working of the technical implement goes, the "desire to understand the world" is there. But the understanding of the world in an ulterior sense has ceased to be desirable because it would not agree with the profitable operations of the machine age.

Concentration upon implements and means had such colossal results that the end, the liberation of the profounder strata of human consciousness, appeared unattractive, anachronistic, and provincial. The sooner it was forgotten, the better. The immediate concerns of mankind grew dutifully so as to keep pace with inventions which anticipated satisfactions before desires were born. An uncanny appetite was hailed as the Olympian thunderer of the twentieth century, making jungles quake and sending the four rivers of paradise back to their sources. Growth is a play around the principle of culmination; a hurricane finds its justification in creating the greatest wave that ever rose from the sea, be it even for a second. Through man the hurricane Life seemed set to bring the wave of its inventive and productive potentialities on the planet Earth up to its maximum. A hypertrophy of the will accelerated the course of business cycles and empires and drove introverts underground. Yet the will, says Schopenhauer, may be fanned to such a degree that intense irritations and tremendous passions result, which then lead the individual not only to assert his own existence but to deny that of others and even to eliminate it where it blocks his way. This is the reverse of the picture. "The fighting male," wrote Benjamin Kidd about 1900,[20] "has turned in our time, bored beyond the last degree of sustenance, from all the problems of the intellect to the gross unimaginative materialism of military and economic war."

Theoretically the industrial civilization founded by the bourgeois is a huge advance over the militaristic practices of the age of feudalism. People are taught that they should use their work as a weapon for advancement. The empire founded on war gives place to the empire founded on trade and production, and a society based on highway robbery is supplanted by a society in which man has a right to accumulate claims by honest toil. We have already mentioned, when we spoke of the decadence of work in Europe, that this splendid theory was shipwrecked, among other things, by the refusal of the globe to grow in accordance with the growth of productive power. Instead of growing it contracted. The middle class expected the masses to remain loyal to its productive apparatus even after this apparatus had ceased to offer advancement through legitimate work. In the emotional sterility of the heartbreak house of the bourgeoisie resentment was discovered. The next step was to see that resentment and its myths of blackmail and violence, which Georges Sorel brought into a system, might be useful as a method of advancement. The last step was to compare the usefulness of resentment with the usefulness of legitimate work as a method of advancement, and to decide in favor of the former method.

One cannot blame the bourgeoisie directly for the disturbances heralded by Schopenhauer and Kidd, whom we have quoted at random. The bourgeoisie is, it appears, perfectly right when it maintains that the martial conflagrations which have taken place under its rule have been flare-ups of the not yet safely entombed atavistic irrationalism of mankind. If all mankind were educated to a point where it resembled the bourgeois—the *homo economicus*, "sublimely gifted with a knowledge of his economic interest"—wars presumably would not take place, because every child knows that "war does not pay." But the child in man does not act accordingly. Indirectly, however, the very theory that economic self-interest is the best available proof of man's rationality and the most beneficent way to run society introduced the fallacy that a man's rational and social worth is demonstrated by the degree of cleverness which he employs in advancing his worldly position.

This doctrine was dangerous for several reasons. In the first place it destroyed the sacred function of work for which Péguy has found such beautiful and nostalgic similes: "So much of their work was prayer, and the work room an oratory." [21] Secondly, by substituting a craving for tangible advancement in a secular civilization for the intangible happiness of self-rewarding work, people who could not offer proofs of their rational and social worth in accepted property terms were made to despise the meager and unrewarding present and to embrace a dynamism of change which possessed all the potentialities for evil as well as for good. In the third place potentialities for evil were enhanced by the fact that the civilization, whose claim to offer equality of opportunity depended on the degree to which it kept expanding, ceased to expand. Because the entrepreneur, the leader of this civilization, needed inexhausible space to keep the profit spiral mounting, he treated space as if it were inexhaustible long after it ceased to be so in any legitimate sense. He needed cheap labor in order to compete, but he also needed customers for his goods; unfortunately, in this case he would have to pay high wages and labour would no longer be cheap. The "natural" solution would be not that he would have to pay the high wages which were needed to give him customers, but that expanding space would furnish the customers—new continents, new Americas, which would need his goods and pay for them with raw materials. In such a situation the assumption of equality of opportunity could be maintained indefinitely through migration to the new spaces.

The ideal order of things from the point of view of capitalism, in which capitalism would never have lost its grip on a generally peaceful and generally progressive world, would have been a perpetuation in the Western world of the circumstances that made England prosper in the first part of the nineteenth century. This perpetuation was impossible because the growth of organic matter, including man, is at all times a hazardous enterprise in the face of determined opposition to growth on the part of inorganic matter; but in the nineteenth century two increasingly maladjusted modes of the physical cosmos, growth and non-growth, clashed for the first time seriously. It so happened that the entrepreneur answered the refusal of inorganic matter to yield new continents by calling in the magic of political controls and tariff walls; this answer gave Lenin the title for one of his most interesting pamphlets, "Imperialism, the final stage in the development of capitalism." The twentieth century has paid the bill with two world wars.

We have suggested that failure to define the machine as a device for the creation of "time for wisdom" has deprived the world of two great advantages which optimists a hundred years ago hoped would be the real product of the newly founded factories: peace, and relief from drudgery. Perhaps we should ask ourselves whether we should not be grateful to a hard generation which sacrificed the emotion that made Europe, and embraced in its stead the science that threatens to unmake the world? The surrender of the world to the dictates of the surface mind was in a sense heroic, like the crippling of the feet of Chinese girls. The victory of technology over dire Malthusian prophesies proclaimed, so it seemed, the possibility of endless quantities of life, and was perhaps worth being paid for by the abandonment of imaginative fullness.

A. E. Housman, in his epilogue, describes how weather-beaten, cunning Mithridates of Pontus swallowed "all that springs to birth from the many-venomed Earth." The king lived on a diet of poisons; and when intriguing courtiers and scheming rivals with an oriental sense for drama "put arsenic in his meat" and "poured strychnine in his cup," Mithridates had nothing to worry about because his stomach was trained for this kind of fare. The roundabout way of the bourgeois was perhaps a training for the unrelieved ugliness of a totally secularized, dehydrated, and antiseptic truth which needed a strong stomach.[22]

Yet two immense wars are hardly convincing proof that the method has been successful. Perhaps the theory that truth cannot be other than ugly, utilitarian, and aggressive is wrong. Perhaps it is wrong to assume that not the whole personality is required to experience truth, but only man in his role as a social adaptation to the moment. In the great wrestling match between physical enlargement—the change of the globe into

## THE MIDDLE CLASS AND EUROPE 47

an industrial plant which keeps two billion people alive—and spiritual enlargement—the development of a consciousness which is concerned with creating a soul for the overgrown body—the industrial plant has been victorious. This victory is wonderful and at the same time empty; like a breakneck drive in a car, it elates in the beginning and is meaningless in the end. We hear of pilots who are one day in Brazil, the next in Africa, the third in Arabia, the fourth or fifth in India, but the vista and the reaction are always the same.

Earth as a physical phenomenon is now controllable but insignificant. There are the facts, and there is nothing to add but resentment. Since they ceased to be symbols, facts are repetitious, and create repetitions. Every step away from the starting point leads back to the starting point; London looks like Shanghai and Chicago like Rio. This is ultimately disappointing even to those who in the teeth of Carlylean and Kierkegaardean and Nietzschean misgivings have heroically atrophied their consciousness, as Mithridates ate poison, in order not to miss the priceless opportunity to inherit the earth. It dawns upon them that this kind of earth is not worth the effort; and through a queer trick of retributive justice man is forced, in order to enjoy his spoils, to give back to the globe through his imagination the poetic air which he killed in the excitement of conquest. The hard fact he insisted upon cheats him in the end, and he has to acknowledge its vanity in order not to be crushed by its dullness.

The poison by which consciousness is scientifically atrophied is familiar to me; I too was coached, unsuccessfully as it turned out, to become a useful member of Western society, a slave of "decomposed time." The poison has a name: education. Education should release, as Plato said, "a health giving breeze from a purer region," and build up a "habit of order" which can become a "principle of growth"; but education in our midst tends to be the transformer of dullness into activity.

Education in Germany before and during the first world war merely built up resistances in its victims that a whole lifetime was hardly enough to dissolve. The students felt like knights errant called upon to prevent the rape of a beautiful princess by a monster. The princess was the world, and the monster the roundabout way which made the philistine master. The students were supposed to eat dust, in order later to eat from golden dishes. In those days of prosperity, before the first world war, one could not argue about it; but now, with all the golden dishes broken, we might as well draw the conclusion that dust will produce nothing but dust.

With every energy in its possession the school interfered with the warm, evolving tradition of European letters—the engagement of all the human faculties in recreating the cosmos, in imitating, as Aristotle put it incomparably, Nature "in sua operatione," in doing like Nature on the level of the spirit. The school interfered with the great age-old solemn habit of recreating the cosmos as an actor recreates a play—consciously, and yet driven on beyond himself by the power of poetry. And we, the students, vainly built up resistance in ourselves, trying to prevent the grand aspect of the world we felt moving in us from being shattered. It was shattered. Not only did the lights go out over Europe twice in one generation, but Europe's monuments became meaningless long before they were laid prostrate by bombs.

By some grotesque mistake the spiritual furniture of bygone days still crowded the curriculum when I was a student. Respectable society used an idealistic vocabulary, as Bernanos hints, in order to have a good pretext to be shocked at the materialism of Marx. If I recall rightly my nine years spent in the Gymnasium, the inspirations which had made Europe suffered transformation at the hands of teachers all too conscious of their duty toward the society which paid them. Take Homer, for instance. Here the ear of the student is supposed to be flattered by rhythms that come from arch-typal times: in

## THE MIDDLE CLASS AND EUROPE      49

Homer the world of today is prefigured by processes and events which have the dignity of symbols, because a uniquely gifted people dared long ago to live Nature as art. To understand Homer well is to remake our present day with a consciousness of its exalted pedigree. What the teacher did, however, was this: He lined up Homeric verses as a boy lines up tin soldiers which he is going to smash with a cannonade of dried peas. The merciless jaws of our memories, directed against the poetical phalanx, were trained to devour it with the blind hunger of locusts settling in green crops. After Homer had been reduced to mere mnemotechnical material—any other pile of words, a telephone directory, would have done as well—the teacher would stand in front of the class, aim a pencil in this or that direction, and start with sinister winking of his brow a deluge of memorized hexameters. The more the Greek class resembled the noise of a shoe factory, the more the victory of the machine age over mythology was assured. With frantic nervousness I waited for the enunciation of my name which would throw me into the crushing processes of the pedagogical mechanism. Whether shoes were fabricated or Homer recapitulated made no difference: everything conspired to kill the little phoenixes of European tradition trying to peep out of the untimely glow of our hearts.

As far as I can remember, education in Germany in the days before and during the first world war was a conspiracy to drive meaning in any absolute sense from the globe. The particles into which the fact of existence was pulverized were allowed to regain meaning only in utilitarian configurations, or to become devices for the training of the will—an abstract will that wanted to "possess" facts in a mechanical sense. Nobody was more surprised than the teachers themselves that an age which could boast of dye trusts and three newspaper editions a day should have recourse to Galilean fishermen and Greek nudes for its edification. Educators accepted the paradox as sheepishly as the next generation accepted Hitler's tenets, which seemed far less paradoxical and far more to the point. The occurrences of spiritual birth were not discussed in the Gymnasium, any more than one mentions the occurrences of physical birth in a Victorian drawing room. The authorities had ruled, taking themselves as models, that success would inevitably be attracted by a ritual which treated the world like a billiard ball, with "every gulf completely closed up," with no shadows left, with every atom weighed, every distance measured, with the world analyzed into hard literal fact, with everything, in short, a huge cliché. War was cliché (*dulce et decorum est pro patria mori*); love was cliché (in Frank Wedekind's first play, *Fruehlings Erwachen*, the love of a schoolboy definitely clashes with the cliché, he commits suicide, and the teachers form a chorus of damnation exulting over the tomb of spontaneity). Cliché mantled like heavy lava the dead volcano of German originality.

According to my impression, actuality never entered the halls of learning as meaning, only as will. Actuality is life, life is a process, a process has no fixed boundaries, and the only things teachers cared for were boundaries, so that a thing might have a front and a hard body to be "accounted for." The goal was death of the emotional content of the world, death of meaning, because if you are surrounded by the spiritual fullness of existence you are inclined to celebrate existence, but you do not regard the world as your potential victim.

The classic description of the problem can be found in Thomas Mann's *Buddenbrooks*. The mental tortures Hanno Buddenbrook was exposed to in school epitomize the experiences of those black sheep who dared, in the face of the precise and unyielding perfection of their elders, to look back from the forbidding renown into which they were led to the consolations which they had expected. Not long ago I saw in New York *Angel Street*, an old-time thriller in which a ghoulish husband is trying mentally to asphyxiate his wife in his Victorian plush catacomb. Seeing this play meant for me living once more, luckily only for three hours, the nine years of my school life. There were the things the husband moved around and concealed, every object as leaden, as frigid, as unconnected, as petty, and as much a denial of infinity and grace as the things which made us die in school before we had lived. Whether an object was in this rather than in that corner, or whether it was by chance in the drawer, mattered like the Last Judgement and weighed on the conscience like eternal damnation. The husband in *Angel Street* had his sinister reasons for driving his wife insane; the teachers had their complexes. Thomas Mann makes one of them kill, or almost kill, what slender academic hopes Hanno Buddenbrook had, because Hanno was the only one who behaved nicely. Under all circumstances the teacher had to assert his superiority, and he picked Hanno because somebody well behaved was bound to be weak and would make no remonstrances.

The modern ice age—"all strife and logic," in Dostoevsky's words—gathered around middle-class education, at least until the first world war exposed the vanity of its pretences. Director Wulicke, head of the school in which Hanno tried to adjust himself to the requirements of his age, "was summoned from a professorship in a Prussian high school; and with his advent an entirely new spirit entered the school. In the old days the classical course had been thought of as an end in itself, to be pursued at one's ease, with a sense of joyous idealism. But now the leading conceptions were authority, duty, power, service, the career. 'The categorical imperative of our philosopher Kant' was inscribed upon the banner which Dr. Wulicke in every official speech unfurled to the breeze." [23] The policy seemed to be one of turning the last possible solace into a threat, which you had to learn by heart in order to dominate it. Otherwise it would crush you. In *Buddenbrooks* it is related how the perspectives and vistas of Job, so dangerous for the conceit of man, were edited so that they would fit the climate of the bourgeoisie; the matter considered worthy of the attention of the students being that "Job had seven thousand sheep, three thousand camels, five hundred yoke of oxen, five hundred asses, and a large number of servants." I may add that the dogmas of religion looked like just another bulging telephone directory. It never entered my mind that religion could have any other function than that of aiding in the back-slapping exercises of man, until I saw the Cathedral of Chartres. Indeed, Chartres was the greatest lesson I received in life.

I have quoted the passage concerning Director Wulicke's activities because it illustrates the harassing of spiritual growth by considerations of career, not because it introduces Prussia as the villain of the piece. The "joyous idealism" of the old days died out not because of Prussia. Its government "in the old days" had been the first to recognize, to consult, and to support the pedagogical genius of the Swiss mystic Pestalozzi. The "joyous idealism" died because it clashed with the exigencies of the machine age. Stefan Zweig, an Austrian, devotes several pages in his autobiography to his school experiences, which were no less synonymous with "compulsion, ennui, dreariness" because they were undergone in Vienna. "I cannot recall a single one of my comrades who would be reluctant to admit that our interests and good intentions were wearied, hindered and suppressed in this treadmill." [24]

Franz Werfel erects a veritable totem pole of terrifying accusations when he comes to the subject of education. "The elders want to clear the youngsters out of the way, unless they can keep them in the role of grateful and docile pupils before their masters. The driving power of our civilization is violence. Our education is nothing but passion and force, sharpened by self-hatred and the recognition in our sons of the faults of our own blood, which then each father punishes in his son instead of in himself." Werfel adds the ominous sentence: "Groaning under the burden of false weights, the soul created for itself false counterpoises." [25] Of the innumerable witnesses who have risen against the disastrous routine of middle-class education as it was practised in Central Europe in the first two decades of this century, I quote only Thomas Mann, Stefan Zweig, and Franz Werfel because they are well known in this country. I give only one comment from outside Germany: "Many men become such that every quality implied by the word heart is atrophied in them. These are the men who have the German view of education, education in facts to the neglect of the imagination, which has fallen heavily upon America during recent decades; part of that killing frost, German kultur, which, during the same decades, fell upon the whole world. It is cankering materialism." [26]

It is a question whether cankering materialism in the first two decades of this century was an article of export of which Germany had the monopoly. The whole world has been sailing complacently over the Styx of spiritual death. We remember what Péguy had to say on the subject of France. Rodin's *Cathedrals of France*, a sigh from the gay heights of sublimity, oscillated between gratitude for an immense artistic inheritance and despair over its destruction by the philistine boring relentlessly from within. There is a characteristic pamphlet by Jules Lemaitre, *A New State of Mind*, written in 1903 during the persecution of the Roman Church by Combes.[27] It has to do with a certain personality that "does not believe in the metaphysical poem that is the Roman dogma." Yet, seeing the persecution in the name of reason of a metaphysical poem, of a "certain hereditary disposition of sensibility," of a certain fashion to "dream the world," he instinctively rallies to a cause which is at the same time "excellent and desperate." He wonders what can make the persecutors so sure that they have a right to persecute. Science and truth? What truth? Evolution? Progress? And he comes to an interesting conclusion: The same republic which persecutes "a certain hereditary disposition of sensibility" fails in its stead to support the citizens morally, fails to foster, if we may use terms employed in this essay, "good emotional habits," the "right quality of happiness." I am not concerned here at all with the details of Lemaitre's argument, pro-royalist rather than pro-Catholic. The destruction without replacement that he attacks, different in detail, parallels in general what was going on in Germany before the first world war.

As to England, T. S. Eliot declared he was impressed by the accumulating evidence of materialism in the fateful decades from which the first world war sprang. If it was not cankering materialism, it was secularization of the already secularized. Discussing a comment on Baudelaire that Arthur Symons wrote in the nineties, Eliot exclaims: "Even in its cadences it conjures up Wilde and the remoter spectre of Pater. It conjures up also Lionel Johnson with his 'Life is a ritual.' It cannot get away from religion and religious figures of speech. How different a tone from that of the generation of Mr. Shaw, and Mr. Wells, and Mr. Strachey, and Mr. Ernest Hemingway." [28] As time advanced into the twentieth century, winter threw off a few more of its disguises, and gathered its cynical storms over the emotional vacuum which the first world war was to shroud with ruins.

E. M. Forster, educated before the first world war, "speaks of the public school system as being at the root of England's worst national faults and most grievous political errors. For, he says, the faults of England are the faults of the middle classes that dominate it, and the very core of these middle classes is the English public school system, which gives its young men a weight out of all proportion to their numbers and sends them into a world 'of whose richness and subtlety they have no conception,' a world into which they go 'with well-developed bodies, fairly developed minds and undeveloped hearts.'" [29]

On the whole England was fortunate: her protests against the soullessness of the machine age received more attention than those educational practices of hers by which this soullessness was propagated. While Germany had the bad luck to be given highly exaggerated credit for improvements in technical civilization, her protests against "cankering materialism" struck the world at large, if it heard them at all, as dangerous and repellent. The revolt against education of the mnemotechnic type manifested in the nineteenth century by Cardinal Newman in his *Idea of a University*, and by Matthew Arnold when he trusted the genius of Oxford to "inspire us to keep down the Philistines in Ourselves," has become a model for gentility in the West; while the protests of the Germans since Nietzsche, far from genteel, have been proportioned to the dimensions of the offense.

"There is a wintry sky over us," wrote Nietzsche in his early period, in *Schopenhauer as Educator*, "and we dwell on a high mountain, in danger and in need.... There is certainly strength there, enormous strength; but it is wild, primitive and merciless. For a century we have been ready for a world shaking convulsion.... We need not be deceived by individuals behaving as if they knew nothing of all this anxiety. They plant and build for their little day.... We live in the Atomic Age, or rather in the Atomic Chaos." Prophetic words today!

One fine morning in early June, before sunrise, I arrived in Bergamo, a provincial town between the Alps and the plain in North Italy where people count their pennies and sprinkle olive oil over their victuals—yet it is a "jewelled city" of many mute seductions and of regal presence. A great dawn floated down gilded steps, snowy peaks, swelling hills, purple castles, pearly villas, and mingled with the gorgeous shadows of the streets. I was walking from the lower to the upper town, while the young sun broke over the scene with that primeval exultation which, some say, once teased the caravan of life from its bed of mud and made the continents pregnant. The morning air washed the insolent and profane physique of the world and claimed the last particle of dirt and dust as its property, trespassing into the remotest domains until, as the Buddhists say of the thought of the enlightened Buddha, there was nothing in the world that was not one with it.

I had learned nothing else in life but to count the objects I met in order to possess them, to spell my appetite, conjugate my boredom, and calculate my advancement. The fact is I took my Baedeker, mapped out a strategy, and inflicted my presence, which became more and more of a burden to myself, upon one piazza, belvedere, and castello after another. Whenever I came to a stop I glanced around, disunited what was one, broke the glittering panorama to pieces, and troubled the great consensus of things with a set of analytical tools which, if they could have been put down in a book, must have looked exactly like my Latin grammar.

Proud moment indeed—to have achieved the goal of the modern world, to be out of tune with the "basic unity of things." If the crowned hills I had climbed with the thoroughness of a mule had been the mountain from which Dante contemplated the actions of the celestial spheres, I still would have crammed the august phenomena into the asset side of a balance sheet. Nothing irked me more than that the great truth "this world is a system of invisible things made visible" [30] dared to persist, though I had obeyed the all too visible world into which I was born and had thrown the key to the invisible into a pool of contempt. I had learned after a fashion to "spell the creation," but I could not read it.

At last I had become a worthy soldier in the roundabout process with all bridges burned behind me, a loyal fragment of that bulky equipment which ever finds its satisfaction by dividing that which is One. Witnessing the sudden transport that had seized the world, I resented the absence of the neutrality of prose, to which I had adjusted myself. I am convinced that ultimately the destruction of Europe can be traced back to universal experience of this kind, to traditions talking too loudly to consciences that decline to listen to them.

I blotted out the walls and towers of the New Jerusalem called Bergamo merely by looking at them, and tried to preserve my self-respect by reshaping the dust into a figure of blind energy. I lived through the moments of dark triumph which must accompany the falling of bombs on cosmos made manifest. That morning I was convinced that the battle against my education was lost, that the days of conformism had begun, that I would drift through my apportioned time a perfect philistine, and, by joining complacently in the surface combinations of my age, that I would at least earn three meals a day and perhaps a surplus for investment in the strategy of the top mind. It was a long time before I heard the far-off horns announcing that the hunt for the Unicorn was still on in the twilight into which the European tradition had faded.

## CHAPTER II

# BIRTH AND DEATH OF THE SPIRIT

> *I was myself brought up by humane People to have faith in a humane God. It was to the highest extent intolerable to me. Ah, Madame, what a revelation, what a bliss to my heart, when, in the nights of Mexico, I felt the great traditions rise up again of a god who did not give a pin for our commandments.*
>
> —Isak Dinesen,
> *The Deluge at Norderney*

In the foregoing chapter I have suggested that the collapse of Europe and the collapse of the European imagination are practically the same thing. It was my intention also to intimate that the exigencies of the machine age were not compatible with the existence of a unifying European imagination, one that moves in the slow time of organic psychological growth—the time for which theologians use the term "kairos" [1] and which Bergson has called duration, existence which endures in our psychological depth. I have tried to indicate that a certain hereditary disposition of the heart to enjoy and appreciate the world from within was artificially killed so that the world might be learned, described, and conquered.

Is it very reactionary to suggest concentration on the rebirth of wisdom, the murdered avatar of time? I think the suggestion is very advanced. So far, our generation has had the bad luck to cash in only a negative interest on the investment which our parents and grandparents made in the machine, namely, world wars. It is legitimate to look out for the positive interest. The machine should enable us, in the security of controlled matter, to draw the liberated spirit into the heart of our communities.

The acrimonious attitude towards the bourgeois evident in these pages is caused mainly by the suspicion that most people in our mechanized world dread nothing so much as to be amply supplied with time for wisdom, and are perfectly content with the "decomposed time" which makes success in the embrace of the moment possible. Attacks on unregenerate fellow beings remind one of the familiar sermons in which the pastor pours his wrath over the few faithful before him because so many faithless fail to show up. To make generalizations about one's neighbour is one of the outstanding vices of the twentieth century, and I wish to make quite clear that it is not my purpose to stop resentment by adding my own resentment to the chaos. All my life I have heard people express the conviction that with the physical elimination of one group or another the rivers would flow again with milk and honey: either it was some hereditary national foe whose disappearance would spell bliss, or it was the capitalist, or the bolshevist, or the Jew. Now it is the German. I hope it is clear that I wish no physical violence, but only the elimination of that kind of mentality which induces us to have notions of physical violence. The foe, like the kingdom of God, is within us.

In the present chapter I shall point out a few incidents in the battle now raging in the mind of the European between two types of consciousness, two types of time, and two types of reason and truth. The heat with which this battle is being fought could be evidence that the claims of the Infinite for a revival in our heart are still good.

It seems appropriate, at this point, to lay down a few definitions on the altar of semantics. The "bourgeois" is a mental case; he pits the quantity of goods he has brought under control against the improvisations of Infinity and considers himself victor. From the point of view of our argument there is no difference between capitalistic and communistic adherents of economic materialism; both exploit "the secular characteristics of the people." [2]

It is of course true that there has never been a society which was not confronted with the problem of satisfying human wants resulting from scarcity of goods. It is a matter of emphasis. In the words of Peter Drucker, both the middle class and its creation and tool, the proletariat, have made "economic rewards the socially significant rewards, economic prestige the socially decisive prestige, economic activity the representative activity of society." [3] I have never understood why society should pick such standards. The unique gift that distinguishes man from animal is consciousness. The cultivation of consciousness and not the cultivation of appetites would seem to be the most rewarding end of human activities. I also have never understood why the reversal of the Platonic scheme of social significance as such has been identified with progress.

The philistine is one who, through lack of spiritual training, has become incapable of hiding the limitations of his particular outlook. The philistine settles comfortably in the boundaries of his special position in society, which is as it should be. But he refuses stubbornly ever to transcend the boundaries in which he is snugly encased; he refuses, and acts out his refusal, to understand his special position as related to a limitless whole. Obviously "philistine" refers to no particular set of activities as "bourgeois" does; any aristocrat, peasant, or college graduate is a philistine if he limits creation to the scope of his job, instead of enlarging his job, by understanding it as part of the action of the Whole, to the scope of creation. Because aristocrats and South Sea Islanders, if they are true to type, *are* rather than have a job, they have a distinct attraction to such wayward contemporaries as are tired of the mania of the bourgeoisie to produce experts.

The term "humanist" sounds much better than bourgeois or philistine; it acquired prestige in connection with the Renaissance, when Western society returned to classical standards which allegedly were formed by making man the measure of all things. A society whose nucleus is the formula "man the measure of all things" is, as we are inclined to believe nowadays, myopic. It is evidence of the discredit into which the formula fell during the nineteenth and twentieth centuries in Germany that brilliant attempts were made, from Nietzsche and Bachofen to Werner Jaeger, to prove that classical standards were not the product of a man-centered society, but of universal forces (the Mothers, Dionysos, Fate). The *clarté* and victorious beauty of Greece presupposed an immersion in the "partial death" of a unifying and intuitive night. Take that night away and the Apollonian glamor that radiates from Greek art and that expresses the denouement of a tension shrinks into a dull statement of external relations like the Greek façades of bank buildings. "Humanists" are attacked here only in so far as they deny the law of alternation between spiritual birth and death, and tend to ignore the margin of depth and darkness in our lives without which the individualized day would be harsh and unbearable. Here then we have the paradox of a theory of dehumanization which purports to be more "humane" than humanism.

Also connected in a sense with semantics is the problem which burdened my conscience in the foregoing chapter: how to leave America out of the debate. America, reproved by many Europeans for having disturbed with her economic pressure the peaceful accents of slower continents. America, whose restless cities do not reflect "kairos"—time which has found fulfillment. I can only repeat what I have already said: In America I am more impressed by the collective action of natural energies, which makes of man a natural force too, than by the splitting up of this collectivity into its individual or class components. Admittedly this picture of the New World is pagan and contrary to what American education aims to accomplish. However this interpretation preserves the character of America as the world's greatest and most successful adaptation of a society to the Unconditioned on the plane of nature. Because it is in flux, America prevents premature crystallizations of consciousness around complacency and resentment. Because it is young, it scorns the slow processes which would sever the consciousness from the daylight of the immediate, and which would accustom it to the regenerative influences of "divine indirections." In my infatuation with the Whole I love America because it is carried along by the unifying vibration of an element.

When I read in Bergson of "the unity of the impulse, which, passing through generations, links individuals with individuals, species with species, and makes of the whole series of the living one single immense wave flowing over matter," I think of America. In America the machine age ran away from the bourgeois, it became a fluid coagulating in unsuspected shapes, a force of revolutionary distinctions, poetic license, and uninhibited directness. "Strange quests enter the scene; the glisten of unknown fish is seen in the net of existence." We read of "a jazz age producing marvels in science, music, and mechanics as bizarre and fantastic as Matisse's in paint." [4] Sinclair Lewis sees an ideal novel "full of the passion for the beauty and stir of life, of people, of rivers, and little hills, and tall towers by dawn and furnace kindled dusk. The novelist will not see life as necessarily approaching the ideals of a life insurance agent. He will see it as a roaring, thundering, incalculable, obscene, magnificent glory." [5]

"America is like a vast Sargasso Sea—a prodigious welter of unconscious life swept by ground swells of half conscious emotions," writes Van Wyck Brooks.[6] "All manner of living things are drifting in it, phosphorescent, gayly colored, gathered into knots and clotted masses...everywhere an unchecked, uncharted, unorganized vitality like that of the first chaos." Waldo Frank's vision is assailed in America by a "rooted tissue of past world heaped on a jungle floor." [7] Thomas Wolfe sings, "Time immutable—the time of rivers, mountains, oceans and the earth." And for Mary Austin jazz becomes the leitmotif in a New World enterprise full of unity and abundance "unharnessing traditional inhibitions," "indispensable to the formation of a democratic society out of such diverse human material America has to work with." [8]

In Europe the emotional consequences of the roundabout way by which the middle class attacked the problem of happiness were totally different. The robes of Europe are woven by emotional habits, the quality of which is testified to by a vibrant procession in stone, color, thought, and work.

It was inevitable that in the long run the Europeans would feel impelled to inquire whether the actuality of "civilized" man was so satisfactory as to warrant the gambling away of a mode of life which was preponderantly an inward act for the privilege of performing an immense quantity of outward acts. And at this point the European discovered with dismay—transfigured into a cry of resounding pathos by Nietzsche—that at the end of the capitalistic roundabout process waited the philistine. The European felt cheated. His continent had changed from Athena Parthenos into a parsimonious scarecrow vigilantly taking her stand next to a telephone. It should not be held against the European that he felt offended at this discovery.

Santayana once defined Protestantism in terms which would much better fit philistinism: "It is convinced of the importance of success and prosperity; it abominates all that is disreputable; contemplation seems to it idleness, solitude, selfishness, and poverty a sort of dishonorable punishment. Swayed as it is by public opinion it is necessarily conventional in its conception of duty and earnestly materialistic; for the meaning of the word vanity never crosses the vulgar heart." [9]

To advance in the dying sun of meaning, as the middle-class society did, was a spectacle that could have been great, like a Shakespearean discourse on the vanity of things; only the middle class insisted that it had eliminated "the meaning of the word vanity," and thus the spectacle deteriorated into a mere exercise of human conceit. Not that plumbing, pills, and quick transportation are mean things—the emphasis made them mean. The facts lost their distance. Bourgeois Cleopatras failed to throw the pearls of progress into the vinegar of vanity to make them dissolve.

James Joyce once said,[10] "I have been too wearied by people asking me to have some more soup in the midst of conversation." Every denunciation of philistinism climaxes in the complaint that soup, the tangible fact, is taken seriously, and the intangible fact treated like the parlour palm which is always in the way but is part of the social etiquette. "Society tolerates, yes, even admires fanaticism in high finance, but deals pitilessly with the same intensity of purpose when it happens to animate the painter," writes Thomas Craven.[11] In Clemens Brentano's farce, *Der Philister vor, in und nach der Geschichte*, the philistines cannot understand why our Lord died

## BIRTH AND DEATH OF THE SPIRIT

for their sins instead of competing with them in a useful way by opening a hat factory in Apolda.

The amazing Constantin Leontiev, the "Russian Nietzsche," groaned while the trumpets of optimism rang through the nineteenth century. "Would it not be terrible and insulting to imagine that Moses mounted the Sinai, that the Greeks erected their beautiful acropoles, that the Romans waged the Punic wars, that the demigod Alexander crossed the Granicus with plumed helmet and fought at Arbela, that apostles preached, martyrs suffered, poets sang, painters painted and knights shone at tournaments only to make it possible that the French, German or Russian bourgeois in his ugly and ludicrous clothes might have a good time on the ruins of all this past magnificence?" [12] It is hardly possible for us to avoid quoting at this juncture Matthew Arnold. "Consider these people, then," he wrote, "their way of life, their habits, their manners, the very tones of their voice; look at them attentively; observe the literature they read, the things which give them pleasure, the words which come forth out of their mouths, the thoughts which make the furniture of their minds; would any amount of wealth be worth having with the condition that one was to become just like these people by having it?" [13]

William James, whose sensitiveness to quality and its decay was not bound by any regional limits, protested no less vigorously against the human shadow world: [14] "If *this* be the whole fruit of the victory, we say; if the generations of mankind suffered and laid down their lives; if prophets confessed and martyrs sang in the fire, and all the sacred tears were shed for no other end than that a race of creatures of such unexampled insipidity should succeed, and protract *in saecula saeculorum* their contented and inoffensive lives,—why, at such rate better lose than win the battle, or at all events better ring down the curtain before the last act of the play, so that the business that began so importantly may be saved from so singularly flat a winding up." Nietzsche summed up our whole argument when he deplored the tendency of man "to take his graceless ease at the first halting place without thought of crowning his progress"—to settle down prematurely in a routine of means.

We are all philistines and like it. Philistinism is the abdication of distance, of loneliness, of grandeur, of insecurity, of passion, of sleepless nights. Pascal, who intended to "murder sleep" in a sense very different from Macbeth,[15] said, "Jesus will be in agony until the end of the world; one should not sleep during this time." It is precisely to get rid of the kind of divine agitation, or agitation with the divine, with which Pascal was obsessed, that we become philistines. To be a philistine is flattering and rewarding, it is relaxing, it is a welcome escape from mystery. Philistinism is the law of gravitation applied to society; its centripetal weight turns the dangerous cluster of illusions of which society exists into reliable and obedient facts. Philistinism is bliss because the riddles of the Universe are as thoroughly extinguished by it as "civilization" is extinguished by music. Only one detail is wrong with philistinism: it is not an adequate expression of man's potentialities. The quality of its happiness is defective.

We have had to listen with patience to the thunder of the foregoing anthology of discontent directed against the camp of social success and respectability. Needless to say, the middle class in its powerful fastnesses has felt by no means compelled to take the jeremiads of its detractors seriously. It has laughed them off. Once it was stung by a particularly irreverent missile, it has had no difficulty in finding drastic epithets for an effective answer. One of these, if Goethe is right, was "godless and worldless monsters."

Goethe, in the sixteenth book of *Dichtung und Wahrheit*, discusses Spinoza. He accuses society of robbing us of our birthright—to live out our nature in its fullness. "Much which

## BIRTH AND DEATH OF THE SPIRIT

is essentially ours we are prevented from realising; we are not permitted to draw from outside what we need in order to round out our personality, but much is urged upon us which is as foreign to us as it is untoward." To this sacrifice of what is original in us for the sake of conformity we are supposed to make a sweet face. Once launched upon the superficial level of the world, we restore our balance by a sort of frivolity which makes us crave new things the moment we have abandoned an old one. "We supplant one passion by the next; we experiment with occupations, inclinations, hobbies and each and all, only to cry out in the end: every thing is vanity." On this superficial level we are saved for a long while from melancholy by our own superficiality, as we witness the dismemberment of what is profound in us; but ultimately we cannot escape the feeling that our efforts and our hopes are vain. "There are only a few who have a presentiment of such an unbearable conclusion and who, in order not to be confronted with partial resignation, resign totally once and for all. These are penetrated by the eternal, ineluctable and basic, they form notions which are imperishable, and which are not annulled by the contemplation of the perishable, but confirmed by it." Because this attitude implies something superhuman and, we may add, asocial, Goethe remarked—in connection with the persecution Spinoza had to endure from the pillars of society—that such persons are usually taken for godless and worldless monsters.

Such godless and worldless monsters continued to live in the capitals and provinces of Europe. To me there is nothing more wonderful in our era—which has seen so much that is wonderful and awful, so many demonstrations running wild courses from the logical to the illogical, so many fertilizations of the will and denials of the divine—than that there should have been delegates of that desiccated Pythian power of Spontaneity living their forgotten lives in the midst of modern loudness. Anatole France says somewhere that if Napoleon had been as intelligent as Spinoza, he would have passed his life in an attic and written a few good books. When Wilhelm von Humboldt visited the battlefield of Leipzig he remarked, "And all the noise is gone, while a good verse lasts through the centuries."

These lasting books, these lasting verses, come in the dark of the night. They are those sudden epiphanies of innocence which Herod failed to massacre, thorough though his Gestapo was. Always there are people who are spoken to by something beyond Herod, people who are blown with the good and bad omens of the stars through dimensions which Herod with all his machines cannot fill. A seeming Nothingness, which is more energetic than a seeming plenty, is obeyed and becomes quality, filtering into matter. The silent interval between the loud spasms of humanity becomes the real person in the drama. The Unfathomable uses as its mouthpiece "godless and worldless monsters," non-conformists, sliding down the slopes of respectability into the hell of public contempt, people whose sensorium blots out a billion-horsepower civilization with music of the spheres.

Here you have the last Mohicans, the last Tasmanians and Patagonians of the Spirit, the lost tribe circling in the void which society denies, and standing in secret communication with a substance which cannot pass the custom house of this society without being loaded, like Homer in school, with purposes and labels and weights making it fit to expire in finality. Here you have the fifth columnists of that Power which, said St. Francis, "chose me because it could find no one more worthless, and which wished thereby to confound the nobility and grandeur, the strength, the beauty and the learning of this world." We are very proud because we found out that two times two is four, and because we divorced the world from its coherence and handed it over to isolation and boredom, to an "intolerable preoccupation with arithmetical abstractions and mechanical instruments, an almost equally abstract interest in the stomach and the sexual organs, divorced from their organic relations."[16] Even the upheavals of the twentieth century, which have their root in the despotism of the very axiom that two times two is four, will hardly convince us that perhaps the axiom is wrong and that mankind's ultimate goal might be an imagination which is the equivalent of a bolder and less rigid concept than two times two is four. The axiom is perhaps wrong not only from the standpoint of Einstein, but also of Dostoevsky: "Twice two makes four is already no longer life, gentlemen.... It is the beginning of death...."

Godless and worldless monsters are those who oppose this death with a very irrational and, in the opinion of the top mind, ludicrous behaviour. There is van Gogh, for instance, doing queer tricks with his physique, interned in one insane asylum after another, mobbed by the good people in whose midst he is trying to live, people amazed at this devilish-looking human engine which loses its tracks once in a while. He has not the university degrees necessary to teach the word of Christ, but by some miracle he transforms his undelivered sermons into colors. There is Francis Thompson, who sleeps in London on or beneath benches, is not permitted to enter public libraries because his appearance shows that he, like Lazarus, walked too far astray from the fleshpots of Dives, is saved from death through starvation by a prostitute (before the Meynells picked him up), and from spiritual frustration "by the traffic of Jacob's ladder Pitched betwixt Heaven and Charing Cross."

There is Nietzsche. People cannot understand that it is not the actual content of his writing, word for word (most of his words contradict each other), which fascinated a certain generation in Germany, but his example—a man actually butchered by normalcy, driven insane by sanity and killed by that common sense which kills every New Jerusalem and Babylon alike which happens to be in its way. Nietzsche is symbolic of the lot of every sensitive—not sensible—person in Europe during the winter of middle-class complacency. Only he went the whole way, he turned his back to the billion horsepower to the point of madness, he danced himself into a solitude that was death.

Maybe it is true that Hitler sent Mussolini on the latter's rather stormy sixtieth birthday a complete set of Nietzsche's works. Picasso once wrote that it is important to know what kind of man painted Cézanne's canvases. If it had been a nice, sociable man in an armchair, a clever manager of the outward circumstances of existence, Cézanne's pictures would have been a fraud. If General von Bernhardi had written the sentences of Nietzsche which Hitler picked up and treated as if they were written by General von Bernhardi, they would not mean a thing besides their obvious implications. The violence in Nietzsche's language was meant to be an antidote to complacency, a parabola of intensity, just as Francis Thompson's and van Gogh's tumultuous non-violence served the same end, just as the devotees of the Zen sect in the Far East shake themselves out of their routine thinking by shocking analogies.

There must be something profoundly irritating in the arrangement of modern life. Destinies are treated as if they were umbrellas; otherwise Nietzsche, Thompson, van Gogh, Strindberg, Gauguin, Tolstoy, Rimbaud, Baudelaire, and a hundred others would not have courted ruin with an assiduity which turned out to be genius. The gap between genius and society should have the attention of the historians of our epoch just as much as Germany's comparative lack of iron ore and Italy's total lack of coal. If we adopt the Kantian formula that genius is Nature working as reason in man, then this gap means that a higher reason, representing the absolute Whole of Nature, the Tao, is opposed to a lower reason, representing society's interest in the utilitarian and instrumental detail of Nature.

The complacent indifference of modern man to the signals from the deep, an indifference which is housed and nursed in the artificial paradise of lower reason, would no doubt be commendable because it has the pleasant property of assuring good sleep. Yet people have nightmares because they "live only half lives," because the bourgeois sophists killed the Dionysian mystery. A basic emotion has been taken away, and people resent this subtle robbery more than an actual robbery at the expense of the outward man. William Blake foresaw a hundred years before Freud that a stoppage of emotional currents breeds reptiles. "If you, who are organised by Divine Providence for spiritual communion, refuse, and bury your talent in the earth, sorrow and desperation pursue you through life.... You will be called the base Judas who betrayed his friend."

We learn that the terrible revolutions against the peace and the sleep of the bourgeois are caused by the envy of those who have not arrived at the comfortable level of the middle class, the have-nots who cannot wait, and refuse to work in orthodox fashion. This explanation is another trick of the lower reason, by which we are happily assured that the root of the disturbances ruining our lives is no more than the commonplace reality of a wage dispute. The abyss beneath our feet is denied. A non-materialistic, psychological interpretation of the almost apocalyptical unrest which has seized the globe is ruled out.

Denis de Rougemont, in his stimulating book, *Love in the Western World*,[17] called the German romanticists about 1800 the "New Albigenses"—a return of the great heresy of the Middle Ages which had revolted in the name of the Spirit against the Sacraments, the "Synagogue of Satan." The oppressive sacraments of the modern age are the facts of the bourgeois code, "satan's Moral Law of vengeance" in Blake's words, the "fear of death" which caused the bourgeois "not to live," as Hofmannsthal cried out in despair as if he, the Apollo, had been flayed by Marsyas.[18] Alas, the ascendancy of the Apollos over the Marsyas has become a pious myth. For fear of death the Marsyas of about 1900 decided not to live in the truth of their innermost nature, but in the applicable truth of their reasoning power, "an abstract, objecting power that negatives everything."

The great romantic plot against the modern priesthood of the mechanized and legalized fact was developed early when the industrial revolution—the Cain who was to kill his brother Abel, the French Revolution and the idea of fraternity—began its defiant career. The two poets who started a kind of holy non-conformism directed against the profanation of the globe by "machinery and commerce and war" were an Englishman and a German, Blake and Novalis. These two souls, springing from the opaque bodies of their nations like water from the rock at Moses' bidding, united in prophecies which only now can be fully understood. Standing midway between Pascal and Nietzsche they represent the arcanum of the European tradition, the evasive and disembodied current of the spiritual light. The minds of the Englishman and the German were moved by the vertigo which once had formed the Cathedral of Chartres. The decadence of this secret energy begot the theory that the only inspiration that "pays" is, next to complacency, resentment. Blake turned against the England of his day: "All the arts of life they changed into the arts of death in Albion." And Novalis turned against the "state factory," built on the brutal power of possessive instinct, reason, and commerce—the Prussia of Frederick the Great and his successors.

From the point of view of their sensitiveness, attuned to an asocial order of things, to a kind of mystical anarchy, the great movement of anti-romantic forces, unloosened by the emancipation of commerce and industry, was tainted with the stigma of death. The nineteenth century, which Blake and Novalis entered as if it were the palace of a joyless, merciless old demon, was prepared to extinguish, for the sake of security, the mysterious fire in the soul of Europe. About a hundred years later Hofmannsthal in the little essay on van Gogh I have already quoted writes: "For months I have met nothing but a deluge of faces obsessed by nothing but the money they had, or the money others had. Their houses, their monuments, their streets, all appeared to me as the grimace, a thousandfold reflected, of their ghostly non-existence." And then Hofmannsthal contrasts with facts which are the furniture of "the eternal nothing, and the eternal nowhere" the facts redeemed by van Gogh. The innermost life of these facts arose from the chaos of non-existence as particles of a new dawn to meet their brother, the artist.

It is easy to point out—in the creed of Blake, Novalis, and other adherents of "thoughts out of season" whom the middle class did not burn at the stake but froze into neglect until their creations, after the death of the creators, happened to fetch a market price—it is easy to point out the anti-human character of this great heresy. And, to be sure, it has been pointed out. Luckily, Law, Reason, and the Machine found defenders. The world of man, the anthropocentric illusion which after all makes it normally possible for us to travel in safety to Paris and the Riviera, defends itself through the humanists against people who assert that the anthropocentric illusion is a perversion of truth for the sake of superficial advantages. They may be superficial, but they are advantages. It is not our duty to analyze these advantages, but to pillory the shortsightedness of the humanists and their deplorable inadequacy in the business of selling their blessings to the world without causing epidemics in the soul.

Characteristic of the counterattack of the humanists against what we have called the New-Albigensian heresy are the responses Nietzsche and Rousseau have evoked. Nietzsche, during the first world war, was made the exponent of Germany's antisocial behaviour. This exploiting of Nietzsche for the ends of political strife not only denoted a considerable lack of perspective, it also was a tactical error in so far as the re-education, the winning over of German youth for the common cause of mankind was concerned.

As I have already indicated, the young people who fought on the German side in the first world war were given clichés as an answer if they asked what they were fighting for. The only thing the German soldier himself knew was that he was not fighting for the bourgeois. It was therefore a singular blunder on the part of Allied propaganda to make Nietzsche, hero of the one significant prison-break which had occurred in German literature between the death of Heine and the dawn of the twentieth century, the representative of Germany's struggle. If this were true, if Nietzsche were really the St. Jago who fought from the clouds with the German armies against the Saracens of prose, German youth had a cause. It was not true. The German armies fought for prose, while Nietzsche was the man of imagination at the time when Bismarck "made Germany great and the Germans small." He, like the German soldier in the first world war who had to find the measure of his sacrifice within himself, was crucified by the smugness of the German philistine. Even the amiable pedants in Basel that Nietzsche called his friends answered his spiritual torments with a polite, and more often with an impolite, yawn.

The great disturbing melody of Nietzsche's message was recognized first by a Danish Jew, Brandes, and by Hippolyte Taine. The German bourgeosie ignored him, hated him. The allied propaganda forged together a kind of bourgeois international against the assertion of the profounder self in man—a momentous mistake. It gave German youth, which was opposed to stuffiness on the home front and therefore loved Nietzsche, a sophisticated pretext to include in its aversion the victorious powers of the West whose avowed business was not to rid the world of the jailer of the Spirit but to establish his rule.

The common cause of mankind is not the bourgeois but the living soul.

Now to Rousseau. It has become the habit to see in Rousseau a kind of dishonorable honorary German, and by hitting Rousseau to hit not only the Wagnerian-Imperialistic-Vitalistic Germany but also one of the expressions of the active, man-dwarfing, man-overriding, naturalistic Whole which was celebrated by romanticism. Rousseau is one of the most dangerous interruptions of the anthropomorphic illusion that "man is the measure of all things." Explicitly and implicitly he attacked the complex, venerable apparatus in which this illusion is enshrined. His enemy was Rome—in Rousseau's case not the literal Rome, which he interpreted to suit his theory that laws ought to be flexible, but the Rome which stands for inflexible legalism, vested interests, abstractions, pragmatism, bureaucracy, institutional rigidity, the "objective," the rational, the concrete, and all the devices that make the abode of man a well-protected fortress against the anarchical manoeuvres of the Infinite. "Plato," he writes in *Emile*, "purified the human heart, Lycurgus, the lawgiver, perverted it." In Rousseau's *Discourse on the Arts and Sciences* we read, "An ancient tradition passed out of Egypt into Greece, that some god who was an enemy to the repose of mankind, was the inventor of the sciences." We know this mysterious god: it was the serpent in paradise.

The humanists who defend the body of occidental civilization against the apostles of anarchy do well in concentrating upon Rousseau. The reputation Rousseau enjoys among the fastidious cannot compare, for perhaps faulty reasons, with that of Blake and Novalis. His pantheistic fits do not seem to lead away from the physical body of Nature and its oppressive fertility; we recognize in his make-up the clouded fires of unredeemed instincts and enthusiasms, the brute growth of strong plebeian plants which choke the object they embrace, just as the Universe "fairly choked" Rousseau. Though he likes to lose himself in space, he encounters not distance but voluptuousness. The manufacture of heavy emotions in German beer gardens, which Romain Rolland describes in *Jean Christophe*, is maliciously placed under the patronage of Rousseau. Both Rousseau and Wagner share the displeasure of Irving Babbitt, whose attacks against romanticism have two obvious drawbacks: that he abstains from sketching an attractive picture of the world of abstract reason which "romanticism" is rebelling against, and that he identifies Rousseau, not an aristocrat in the kingdom of emotions, more or less with the whole movement.

Though of cruder stuff than Blake and Novalis, Rousseau's elucubrations were of much greater consequences in the world of facts than the esoteric reflections of the Englishman and the German. The nineteenth century has no aspect which cannot be traced back to Rousseau. The citizen of Geneva is made responsible not only for the anarchical German music which "extinguishes civilization," but for totalitarianism in every form. This is the reason we treat him here—because the change from the responsible to the irresponsible we have witnessed in our time naturally cautions us against acceptance of any kind of philosophy which explodes the tangible footholds of convention for the sake of spontaneity.

We learn that Rousseau is the father of totalitarianism because he made "general will" the sovereign over our political destiny—which means that any Robespierre who is convinced that he represents the general will, will feel entitled to punish a deviation from the party line with the guillotine. The general will is an irrational mystical concept, spontaneously evolving and constantly breaking the laws which try to fetter it for the sake of individual interests. Against the objectivity of the law, general will pits the subjectivity of its ceaseless self-assertion, but in another sense it represents a higher kind of objectivity, the dynamic principle of life as such which shatters the dead weight of legal pedantry.

BIRTH AND DEATH OF THE SPIRIT 77

A dangerous doctrine indeed, where revolution and reaction meet. There is no autocracy which could not avail itself of a Rousseau thus interpreted. An apologist of Czarism, Pobedonoszew, procurator general of the Holy Synod, uses Rousseauistic terms to bolster up the mystic authority of his lord and master—in this case not general will but the emperor of Russia: "All laws are an abomination because they limit the free will of the supreme ruler and his agents." [19] Worse still, the general-will concept hands ammunition to Nazi ideologies. It is only a small matter to identify the people with God, or rather God with the Fuehrer, who, "by virtue of his supernatural qualities and the intrinsic strength of his mission, is able and qualified to express the real or objective will of the people. The people's will is considered erroneous and invalid if it fails to coincide with the Fuehrer's will." [20]

But, if the anthropocentric purists are thus enabled to link naturalism in its romantic version to certain poisonous forms of statecraft, Rousseau can be made patron saint of laissez-faire liberalism, the gospel of the bourgeoisie, too. It is clear that at the time when Rousseau wrote the *Social Contract*, the bourgeois—eager to create with his pent-up energies the epic of industrial expansion—saw in the theory of the general will a parable which told the story of his own will encountering feudal restraints. "Man," wrote Rousseau, "sewn in a straitjacket at birth, nailed up in a coffin at death,—so long as he retains human form he is chained by our institutions." In those days it was the bourgeoisie which shouted with Rousseau, "We approach the state of crisis and the century of revolutions." [21] Then institutions were anathema, today they are inviolable. Then, drunk with potential energies, bent upon starting the power age as a child starts a fire, the bourgeoisie interrupted the minuets of the nobility with "direct action"; now—I am speaking of conditions which provoked the psychological upheavals in Europe—the bourgeoisie, conventionalized and counting its rights and privileges, denounces the advocates of originality and vitality as disciples of Rousseau, and throws them into the same pot with racial cranks and political irrationalism in general.

It is interesting that the anti-romantic Irving Babbitt himself was slightly dismayed when noticing the progress towards goody-goody senility within the body of the middle class. "A year or so ago," he writes in the preface of the *New Laokoön*, "I chanced to be strolling along one of the narrow streets that skirt the Quartier Saint Germain, and came on a bookshop entirely devoted to reactionary literature; and there in the window, along with books recommending the restoration of the monarchy, was the volume of M. Lasserre and other anti-romantic publications." Lasserre wrote a very readable book in the humanistic, that is Babbittian, tradition, in which he arranged romanticism with detached airs. He blamed it for "sublimating and exalting the aspirations and egoistic voluptuousness of the individual sentiment." One wonders whether this is not precisely what an aristocrat would have said of the eager Rousseauistic bourgeois in the eighteenth century. Then it was the middle class which took pride in being capable of perspiring in the cause of individual promotion, and longed to get rid of the taboos imposed by the impersonal and almost Confucian ritual of the Ancien Régime. Now it is the middle class which has grown a feudal armour for protection against the barbarian fervor of the eternal Rousseau who, as history proceeds, keeps breaking through one layer of privilege after another.

Unlike Lasserre it was not monarchy which Babbitt defended when attacking Rousseau, but puritan decorum. There is something direct and plebeian about Rousseau: return to the warm generative mire of existence is indeed a dissolvent of style. But how is it possible to attack Rousseau on this account from the point of view of the middle class, whose lucrative operations were the most merciless dissolvent of style ever to emerge from the hell in which selfhood burns?

With the help of science, the middle class dissolved style all over the globe—because the slow beat of style interfered with the quick operations of self-promotion. Now, after a rule of one hundred and fifty years during which the culture of six millenniums has been pulverized, it attacks Rousseau for having prepared the way. No new style of its own is the point of departure for this discriminating gesture, but rather the autumnal reserve with which an organism, grown old, contemplates the exuberant passion of its youth. Babbitt stands—in a masterful way, and indeed, so far as his personal expression goes, with "style"—for "standards and discipline, virility and seriousness." "With him [Rousseau]," he writes, "begins that revulsion from the rational, the attack on the analytical understanding, on the 'false secondary power by which we multiply distinctions,' which pervades the whole romantic movement." The false secondary power indeed, the lower reason, the top mind—that dearest possession of the middle class!

The French Baron Seillière, who wrote illuminating books on the subject of Neo-Romanticism, calls D. H. Lawrence "Rousseau réincarné." Neither Rousseau nor D. H. Lawrence was seraphic. Both are tainted with the boundlessness, lawlessness, and dangerous directness of Life. But if we hear of the "great dragon Cosmos," a Rousseau-Lawrencean superbird of naturalism emerging from an unredeemed demoniac creation and endangering the abodes of society, we wonder whether the success of such an animal has not to do with the mental Ash Wednesday and herring of middle-class civilization. No doubt much can be said for middle-class civilization, but it is not too well said. If this civilization is to survive it needs to be better promoted; to level accusations against the formlessness of Rousseauism and to make it responsible for the fatal political irrationalism of Europe is not enough if one is bound up as badly in formlessness and technical ennui as is the middle class.

The humanists are not only faced with the dangerous Rousseauistic spontaneity of naturalism but with a spontaneity of the Supernatural too. For argument's sake the simplification may be permitted that the anthropocentric purist took care to drive the essence of religion, which means relatedness, from the face of the globe and retained its legal aspect only, because he preferred to relatedness the counterpart of the Newtonian world machine—that is, the particular social organization which protects unrelated units called individuals. Civilization in this sense breaks up the world into "stills" which need as complement a type of man who is emotionally and imaginatively a "still" too. Thus civilization becomes the Chinese wall, the Maginot Line defending the illusory permanence of an abstract security. Civilization is in this sense a kind of Apollonian reservation which interrupts the wide-flung rhythm of Dionysian possibilities, a great solid shell hiding in an ocean of spontaneity an assortment of carefully labeled museum pieces—well-defined individuals who, in order to enjoy the pride of their distinctiveness, have drained the unifying drug of original life from their veins.

Charles Maurras, for instance—now imprisoned as a collaborationist—is not interested in the Christian inspiration as such. Like Symmachus and Celsus, adversaries of the church fathers Prudentius and Origenes, and, as Thibaudet remarks, like Julian Apostata, he sees in the supernatural aspect of Christianity a prelude to anarchy, something vague, disorderly, chaotic, Lutheran, and deadly. But he accepts the Roman Catholic ecclesiastical apparatus, he admires the "cortège of councils and popes," the artificial paradise of ritual and tradition, the legal instruments of spiritual coercion. Christianity as an emotional torch kindled by the Holy Spirit displeases him; but when it is civilized into a bureaucracy he is content.

"Aye, the sea is the Church," proclaimed St. Ambrose,[22] "which pours forth from its doors in waves the crowds of the faithful, and echoes with refluent waves of the people's prayer,

BIRTH AND DEATH OF THE SPIRIT 81

with the responses of the psalms, the singing of men, of women, of children, a crashing surf of concordant song. And what of the wave that washes sin away? And the life giving breezes of the Holy Spirit?" The utterances of this Christian Swinburne are not to the liking of Maurras; but when the church is organized by the Jesuits in Paraguay into a theocratic chain gang, it is to him a model for the world government of the future.

What it really amounts to, however, is that Maurras suggests combating the unifying arts of profundity with a kind of objective top mind, a mechanical order and sacramental pedantry against which the Albigensians of all ages have united their prayers and their songs. Maurras hates the German "soul"; but he admires the "matériel" of Germany, the colossal administration of the physical fact, the "Roman" element in her constitution, the element of control. Now we realize that a loyalty towards pure spontaneity of the Spirit, is, if not permitted to act upon the fact by which human beings are surrounded, only a potentiality that remains outside the test of human actuality. It is formless too, just like the naturalistic heresy. But again it must be said that we have had too much of the human actuality, too much of the organized phalanx of sovereign facts which protect the comfort and complacency of the individual against the sweet and dangerous propaganda of the Whole, touching the earth like wayward strains that pour down from the music of the spheres.

At random we choose an illustration from a popular history written by Harry Elmer Barnes. Barnes, like Maurras, sees Rome's significance come to an end when it ceased to "multiply distinctions." Barnes calls it mental collapse when the imagination, tired out by the oppressive density and closeness of things, tried to reach out, aided by Neo-Platonism, toward its more spacious patrimony beyond the contraction of materialism. He is quoting [28] the formidable Wilhelminian positivist, Adolf von Harnack, who is reported to have told the Kaiser, already burning deep in the hell of selfhood, that one captain of the guard in shining armour was worth more than all German professors together. Although jokes at the expense of German professors are usually enjoyed, the context makes this one sound false.

Harnack is quoted by Barnes because he wrote, in his *History of Dogma*, that "the contempt for reason and science, and these are contemned when relegated to the second place, finally leads to barbarism." This may be perfectly right so far as it goes, but it needed not to be stressed at a time when Europe was about to crash through the thin ice of reason and science, over which it danced as if on solidity itself, into the shame and shambles of the first world war. Furthermore, was anything more unsurpassably barbarian than the pretentious body of Rome, built up by reason and science, a body which required an endless stimulation of appetites in order to find ever new excuses for gratifying them? What else, the Romans seemed to argue, could have been the meaning of organizing the world, but that "the kings should commit fornication with Rome and the merchants of the earth should wax rich through the abundance of her delicacies." The two scholars I have mentioned remind one a little of the merchants who, according to Revelation, watch the fall of Babylon, and weep and mourn over her, "for no man buyeth their merchandise any more." What else, the mournful merchants seem to ask, could have been the significance of centuries of Roman progress but building up appetites which were apt to be gratified not with mere water and goat cheese, as in the sober beginnings, but with tongues of nightingales and with fish fattened by the flesh of slaves? What else could be the end of civilization but to translate everything into atoms of the market, and boost the craving for the "stable, durable, portable, divisible and cognizable" metal which commands the goods of the market, to the degree of an exclusive obsession? Petronius, in his *Satirikon*, makes the rich Eumolpus draft a will in which his heirs

## BIRTH AND DEATH OF THE SPIRIT    83

are "required not to touch their booty till they have devoured his remains before the people." "Close your eyes and fancy that instead of devouring human flesh you are swallowing a million of money!"

An enormous structure, Rome, had been raised through the toil and bravery of countless generations, but the result looked horrible to the author of Revelation as well as to the author of the *Satirikon*. Both St. John on Patmos and Petronius found that the civilization of Rome was a prison with walls so thick no escape was possible except by flight into one's weaknesses. St. John calls Rome the habitation of devils, and the hole of every foul spirit, and a cage of every unclean and hateful bird. Weaknesses kept the market alive, and weaknesses were the only justification one could think of for flattening the world through the weight of Roman organization until it was at last adjusted to the speculations of the bourgeois Trimalchio, whose orgies Petronius has immortalized. But there was no weakness so great that to flee into it could banish the *taedium vitae*.

> On every tree hangs boredom, ripening to its fall.
> But, come, regale us with appropriate detail,
> Those disillusions weeping at the fountains, say,
> Those new disgusts, just like their brothers, littered stale—
>
> Those women. Say, the glare, the identical dismay
> Of ugliness and evil, always, in all lands,
> And say Love too—and Politics, moreover, say,
> With ink-dishonored blood upon their shameless hands.[24]

This civilization—spreading "identical dismay of ugliness and evil" in all lands, revolving around a question mark, and trying desperately to find an answer through the "false secondary power" of analysis—could not have lived on and on merely on the strength of gadgets invented by reason and science. A Scotch professor, after a visit to the ruins of Minoan

Crete, said, "The moral of Knossos is that good plumbing will not save a civilization." Roman civilization became beautiful only as a ruin, when it towered over Gibbon like a thought. When it received the mark of death's infinitude, its obtrusive sanitary and engineering features, its self-conscious temples and trivial circuses—whose false, crowded rhythm is horribly carried into our own time through the monument for Vittorio Emanuele—ceased to be finite and calculated, and no longer concealed vaingloriously the long silent shadows in the human tragedy. They became letters in the drama by which Creation, fanned out in unholy rapture, unifies itself again. They no longer resist unification.

For having spiritualized civilized "non-existence" by fastening its wearisome plurality to the One, as Nature fastens the farthest, coldest, darkest planet to the redeeming Sun, Neo-Platonism is severely censured by Mr. Barnes. The Neo-Platonic writers Emerson used to read in the thin air of New England mornings in order to get "attuned," prepare us, says Barnes disapprovingly, for the Christian thinkers. Yes, the accents of the *Enneads* of Plotinus, preparing the propagation of the Gospels, were needed to deliver man from man, and to make him unravel in the night of a supernatural presence the tissues which he had woven in the daylight of his conceits.

"The earth at peace," say the *Enneads*,[25] "the sea at peace, and air and the very heavens waiting. And let it be conceived how the Great Soul streams inward at every point into that world at rest. The soul, when it enters into the body of the heavens, gives it life and immortality and awakens it from sleep. The cosmos...becomes a blessed living being.... The soul encompasses the heavens and guides it to its own purposes. By the power of this Soul, the manifold and variegated heavens is a unity, through Soul this universe is a god."

Neo-Platonism prepared the City of Rome for the Christian thinkers, says Barnes—Christian thinking meaning surrender, per se the most anti-civilized, or rather a-civilized, act possible.

The famous Neo-Platonist who wrote under the name of Dionysius, himself a Christian, stated "in words which are writ large in the annals of Christian ecstasy": [26] "Attainment comes only by means of this sincere, spontaneous, and entire surrender of yourself and all things." Surrender, a different kind of weakness, an apostolic weakness, was to Christian Platonists the only possible escape from "non-existence." It is the end of civilization, and therefore, for very good reasons for which we have the greatest respect, it is not liked by Mr. Barnes. And yet, these Neo-Platonic and Christian thinkers gave the real answer to the great question why people should have shaped a huge administrative, linguistic, and economic unit called Roman Empire.

The reason was obviously not to gratify the taste of Trimalchio—not to pyramid artifice upon artifice until vomiting spells caused by peacock feathers gave to the surfeited constitution the relief of its original zero—but to prepare indeed for the advent of Christian thinkers, to be a *praeparatio evangelica*, to conduct through the means of civilization to the four corners of the world an inspiration which, like music, would extinguish that civilization. Many a Harnack and Barnes eighteen hundred years ago had good reason to tremble since the ships from Africa and Syria carried to Rome not only the instruments of civilization, monsters for the circus and lobsters for the dinner, but also the apostles destined to drown "the woman which sitteth on seven mountains" in the blood of their martyrdom.

Ruskin complained that the progressivists of the nineteenth century boasted of telegraph and telephone "to talk at a distance when you have nothing to say though you were ever so near." But one wonders whether even Ruskin, if he had lived eighteen hundred years earlier, would not have preferred to charge the facilities of the Roman communication system with the transmission of remarks about the weather rather than with Christian thoughts which, undomesticated, were liable to melt civilization as Semele melted in the presence of Zeus. History teaches us that any thought of magnitude cannot be but dangerous because it cannot but transcend civilization. The church fathers were told that nice people refused to be Christians; that there was nothing in monotheism which could not be said, and was not already said, correctly; that the Christian desire to surrender their identity was shocking.

The church fathers answered that nice people stayed nice and continued their exercises in correctness, but disreputable people who became Christians changed their complexion. All their "Christian blood hymned fervently"; they were "the wheat of God, they panted for the day when they should be ground by the teeth of wild beasts into the pure bread of Christ." Evidently it was not a question of being nice and correct, but of becoming a pioneer of eternity, as it were, an eternity which was blotted out by nicety and correctness until it could no longer be blotted out, until it created its human media, until it seized quite inconsequential people, as the vision seized Bernadette in Lourdes, and transformed them into pillars of fire. Eternity, the great enemy of civilization, picked people here and there, in the streets, in the kitchen, in the brothels and the slave quarters, but also occasionally—strange phenomenon —in the halls of learning, and gave them new eyes. Like Tao, it flowed through the interstices. It projected into the hearts of commonplace men and women its constellations and the play of comets and shooting stars, mere hints of its power presented on the tip of its finger, and made these commonplace men and women wild with a nostalgia for perspective which all that heavy matter of the Roman Empire had obstructed.

The humanists are right to call this a delusion, but the immense space of the spirit was so suddenly and so overwhelmingly revealed that those who had been confronted with it were precipitated into the great permanent sunrise of heaven by a kind of inverted gravitation, against which the attractions of the earthly city counted nothing. In the overflow of spiritual energy which swept these people out of their ruts, only the extreme of Space open to mortal man, namely Death, counted. Though Christian inspiration eventually turned back to Earth, and deposited the accent of Eternity on the objects and subjects of creation by painting them with the color of Love, we are dealing here only with the first mad rush into the boundless bosom of Night—a recurrent, and by no means only a Christian, phenomenon. A Mohammedan general addresses the Syrians, "I send against you men who are as greedy of death as you are of pleasures." The Russian Rozanow writes, "Eternity and I are incompatible; but Eternity—I see it, and as for me, I am a mere phantom." This is good Albigensian philosophy. Eternity is the agency through which the phantom Man recovers his reality.

Primitive Anglo-Saxon chieftains were smitten with the fantastic Christian lore as if with an infirmity.[27] "The kings broke down; power lost its value and had not yet found its significance. Those who for a long time had resisted the fire now did not know how to manage it and abandoned themselves to it until it devoured them. For in the innermost core of Faith is destruction which cannot be mastered but by Love and the office given by God." The destructive radiance of Faith found its victims unprepared. They had no tools with which to subdue the dragons and lions of Eternity when the cage was suddenly opened. The humanists therefore say, "Don't open it; it is bad for decorum." By suppressing the *frisson*, the "shudder which is mankind's best part,"[28] they defy the inverted gravitation which would hurl them beyond themselves into an emotional current not of their own making.

The humanists therefore double the weight of institutions which, like the unwieldy armour in which the crustaceans wrapped themselves at the dawn of life, protect them against the monstrous invention of infinity. This is bad policy. There can be no doubt that the humanists have a good cause to defend—a good, sound limitation; only their policy is bad. By making civilization hard and unyielding, they create a psychological vacuum into which the deluge of Eternity will break unorganized and destructive as with the first Christians. People have to be accustomed to an intercourse with Eternity. They must see it expressed in their institutions and in their cities rather than suppressed, lest they turn savagely against matter and smash its impotent ornaments in quest of what they vaguely feel must be the concealed truth.

In the light of human postulates, the basic formlessness and lawlessness of both natural and supernatural spontaneity, if entirely divorced from the carapace of civilization, has to be admitted. Is it possible to combine the elements into a form which prevents utter anarchy and at the same time prevents, as Blake said, the "breeding of reptiles in our minds"? Let me approach the problem with a few words on a book by Wyndham Lewis, *Time and Western Man*,[29] a book which reflects in a puzzling way certain trends which were particularly prominent in the pseudo-pacific interlude between 1918 and 1933. It is a valuable statement of the position of the disgruntled humanist, presented in a language which one would ordinarily expect to be employed in defense of sophistication; but the author, angered by certain Albigensian outbursts against the "gross specialised values of the mere practical man," summons his talents to rescue the sovereign fact from the witchcraft of total aspects. Frank Arthur Swinnerton[30] informs us that because Lewis "sees all sorts of other men scratching each other's back, and rolling each other's logs, he shouts in holy horror at the spectacle."

*Time and Western Man* lumps together almost everything which used to solace the Neo-Albigensian who was groping for perspective while exposed to triumphant limitations. In the centre of objectionable phenomena we find Bergson, who split Time into alarm-clock time "whose moments are strung on a spatial line" [31] and into psychological time of true duration, and who opposed duration, the threshold of Unity, to the multiplicity of space. Wyndham Lewis poses as a classicist, in the very limited and perhaps untrue sense in which the wounded German imagination after the defeat of 1918 had defined the term, rather maliciously identifying it with the kind of unrelated practicality which, the German tried to convince himself, had won the first world war.

Though Lewis deals only with Spengler among post-war Germans, his book is really a trumpet blast in honor of the English middle class and in defiance of fancy notions by which the defeated powers, not yet able to rearm in actual fact, endangered the sober outlook of the British lion. By boldly calling himself a classicist, which in Germany after 1918 was almost as suicidal as to have a non-Ayran grandmother was under Hitler, Lewis proved truly patriotic. In Germany one was baroque, Proustian, Joycean, Bergsonean, and was given to child cult, abnormal psychology, Cézanne, Russian ballet, Futurismo, or one was nothing. By attacking all these dangerous passions Wyndham Lewis seemed to imply—though he perhaps does not expressly say so—that they were intangible weapons threatening Anglo-Saxon common sense while the tangible weapons were not yet ready. As an aside I may mention that in Germany the guardians of the militaristic tradition, eager to give a *weltanschauliche* basis to their unbending political convictions, believed that the visits to Germany of exotic sages like Tagore were instigated and paid for by the British Government in order to induce the German mind to look for a place in the sun in the future not so much in the proximity of tangible British interests, but rather, as Madame de Staël had already suggested, "in the air."

Lewis was grieved to see "the beautiful objective, material world of common sense" disappear under the accumulation of memories engendered by the Bergsonean concept of duration, the way the castle of Sleeping Beauty vanished beneath an enchanted rosebush. Sleeping Beauty's castle is civilization, a spatialized world hewn out of the original unity of the Universe but, because of the humanists, not permitted to return into that unity. The humanists do not permit civilization to sleep, it must be wide awake all the time. "For the objective world most useful to us, and what may be the same thing, most 'beautiful,' and therefore with most meaning, and that is further to say in a word with most reality, we require a space distinct from Time." But now the rosebush comes, duration, an indefinible process of consciousness, and breaks down the distinction between thing and thing, and individual and individual, "in a confused plurality of interpenetrating terms." Time, "the soul of space," battles Lucifer, rebellious matter that thrives on selfhood.

Space is put to dream in the mighty embrace of Time, its soul, its god. "Space is rapidly, under the guidance of a series of Bergsons, each Time obsessed, becoming the Nothing of the modern European." This is Wyndham Lewis' thesis, and were it so, were the "modern European" not in reality a literary coterie in Chelsea during the twenties which was antiimperialistic for the benefit of their deeper selves, we would not have had a second world war. Actually the war of Space eclipses the peace of Time because the modern European, outside the avantgardists of the Whole whom Lewis attacks, has remained thoroughly loyal to the spatialized aspect of things: the world is cluttered with spatial objects which are either attractive or antagonistic, either plus or minus; the modern European either tries to annihilate them or tries to embrace them, which is often the same thing. He constantly thinks it his duty to react, like animals in Walt Disney's cartoons, either sweet or sour, without ever plunging for a change into the deep current of Time which makes, as Lewis says, a "nothing" of the spatial, solid, exclusive, distinct, and substantial objects he craves. Though the habit belongs to another age, collecting empires is still the great fashion.

Wyndham Lewis, coming from a race of empire builders, is shocked because from the point of view of Bergsonism the space of which these empires are composed is "nothing." He sees quite clearly that the implications of the Bergsonean time concept are immeasurably radical. *Sub specie aeternitatis* there is no difference between a davenport and an empire. The Zen monk is asked, "What is the final truth?" "The screen around the washroom," he answers. Screen, washroom, davenport, and empire belong to the same continuum, the same total event.[32] This is the height of egalitarianism, so it seems. The world of Bergson, says Lewis, has "no favoured moments, no peaks; he substitutes for them a cluster of events or of perspectives, which shade off into each other and into other objects to infinity." This is after all the famous proposition of modern art, which turns out apples and Madonnas with the same innocence of mind, enveloping every object with the rhythm it gathers, consciously and unconsciously, and with more or less talent, in the depth of time. In opposition to the "spatializing instinct of man," which is belittled and discredited by Bergson, is placed, says Lewis, a belief in the organic character of everything. "Dead, physical nature comes to life. Chairs and tables, mountains and stars, are animated into a magnetic restlessness and sensitiveness, and exist on the same vital terms as men. All is alive: and, in that sense, all is mental."

The great anti-Albigensian and sacramentalist from Chelsea protests against a world view which starts from the Whole and refuses to see, even in the most insignificant object, anything but the Whole. This world view is truly cosmopolitan because its character makes it impossible to assert that "East is East and West is West"; on the contrary, "Orient und Occident Sind nicht mehr zu trennen." It is the European tradition of the Fourth Gospel, of the Holy Ghost, secularized into terms which are almost identical with those of the Zen philosophy. In opposition to it Wyndham Lewis, like Charles Maurras, is addicted to the "matériel" of civilization, the legalistic apparatus, the organization of distinct facts into a Whole of its own material order, an organization whose boundaries do not ultimately coincide with the boundaries of the Universe, but which is a kind of tumor on the body of the world —a tumor which has gained autonomy, a workable utilitarian abstraction which claims exclusive loyalty from those who are pressed into service—often against their will or merely because they are born into a certain environment. He likes a gigantic abstraction expressed in timetables and telephone directories and sometimes in ballistics and logistics by the ingenuity of man in order to keep individual egotisms intact— a wonderful and terrifying crystallization of what is really a process of dissociation. Wyndham Lewis would have joined the anguished chorus of Celsus and Symmachus when they denounced in the name of Roman civilization the magic wave of Christianity. It is even possible that he would have joined the crusades against the Albigenses in the Middle Ages and would have sent Joan of Arc to the stake because she had listened to celestial messages before they had been censored by the bureaucracy. He assumes the role of Dostoevsky's Grand Inquisitor, who is forced, out of respect for the humanist code, to crucify the Logos for the second time, because the Word Incarnate is the great dissolvent of social distinctions. Indeed, the humanist is forced to crucify the Universal in every mode, because the Universal cannot be but superlatively egalitarian or, on its own level, fraternal; he must crucify even the universal meaning of Death and Resurrection in order to prevent the submergence of his more specific interests in a common pool of hope.

Obviously it would be quite out of place here to discuss the great spiritual heresy which Wyndham Lewis groups around the time concept of the arch-offender Bergson. It might be exceedingly debatable whether the time concept, or rather the concept of duration, can really serve, as Lewis suggests, as a common denominator for world views as varied as those of, for instance, Abbé Bremond, Jacques Maritain, Professor Whitehead, Professor Alexander, and Oswald Spengler. A critique of Wyndham Lewis' ideas on the subject is, however, not our concern. The whole matter is referred to here for two reasons: We are faced with another telling formulation of the rational and anthropocentric citizen's exclusive faith in the empirical fact which has permitted the growth of our civilization, a position which is shared by the great majority of Occidentals living at the present time; and secondly this formulation, though published as early as 1928, is tinged with a militant note, and through the inclusion of Spengler in the argument, even with a political note. Against this we maintain that politics has nothing to do with the problem. The problem is a-political, it has to do with modern occidental civilization as such, and with the possibility that through rethinking its terms a better psychological balance among its members might eventually be arrived at. But there is the danger that any attempt to replace two incomplete psychological attitudes which have proven effective in the shaping of the modern world—namely, the complacency of the bourgeois and the resentment this complacency has elicited—by a consciousness whose source is not inside society, will be attacked as a kind of fifth column planted by the fake-irrationalism of the Axis in the camp of the victorious, and "rational," Allied Nations.

Partly to combat this possible misapprehension the present essay is written; but instead of following Wyndham Lewis into a discussion of the various philosophies he attacks, I would rather pursue my main point by putting the question whether social practicality is not much better served by practices that support the health of the soul, even though we have to transcend society for this purpose, than by repeating the practices which have disrupted the deeper unity of society. The spiritual phenomena Wyndham Lewis mentions, though they might make strange bedfellows at first sight, have indeed something in common—the attempt to quicken a dead, isolated substance through the alchemy of relatedness. They cannot breathe without the Absolute in the next room, or preferably in the same room, inside their own system. They cannot live without seeing and feeling the knowing smile, the *coincidentia oppositorum*, in which the Universe and its parts meet. "There lives the dearest freshness deep down things." To perceive the emotional charge in things, their implied genealogy, to see them not as fixed points but as the crest of "waves of organization," not in the flat dimensions but in the maze of measurable and immeasurable dimensions—this is a power and an art, the only art that counts. Do we face immanence, or do we face transcendence? Like the Atman and the Brahman, like samsara and nirvana, at one point, the deepest, immanence and transcendence are one in the propitious climate of the Whole.

Undoubtedly, this approach is highly romantic. To discover in an object an "interlocked plurality of modes" and to give it a baptism of "Wholeness" through what Whitehead calls "prehensive unification," is an art which can only flourish in a happy emotional climate. It is romantic because this kind of quest for truth is based not so much on rational as on emotional perfection, on good emotional habits, on a good quality of happiness. Now Whitehead, in his famous lectures in *Science and the Modern World*,[38] is of the opinion that we can train our imagination or creative initiative towards that totality of contemplation which ultimately will make the right emotional integration inevitable. This suggests a kind of yoga that starts by thinking with the brain and ends by thinking with the whole man, which is the same for right feeling:

> Denkt er ewig sich ins Rechte
> Ist er ewig schoen und gross.

There is hardly a more hopeful turn of Whitehead's eminently hopeful reflections than his boldly applying his theory to the banal objects of the contemporary scene. There is nothing banal, nothing insignificant, because everything, rightly seen and felt, is actual; on the other hand there are "no favored moments, no peaks." "To create a little flower," says Blake, "is the labour of ages"; and these ages work on everything, everything is an expression of these ages. Everything is charged with Eternity.

There is still left, however, the hierarchy of opaque and lucid states of mind. The glow bursting from the created world for which the most sublime metaphors have been found by religious mystics can be anticipated in the most everyday matter, if only we can bring ourselves to enter into it by a mental process by which the intuition of the consummate sage is prefigured. The scientist Whitehead turns to the factory: "A factory, with its machinery, its community of operatives, its social service to the general population, its dependence upon organising and designing genius, its potentialities as a source of wealth to the holders of its stock is an organism exhibiting a variety of vivid values. What we want to train is the habit of apprehending such an organism in its completeness." [34]

The idea as such does not differ from the ideas of symbolists —of Maeterlinck, for instance—but if a *homo literatus* had written it, it would be shelved as the emotional unreality of the professional dreamer. It is important to hear a scientist say something in favor of impractical and disinterested truth. "Science," Constantin Leontiev once wrote, "must develop in a spirit of profound contempt for its own utility." What Whitehead really wants is to train little Goethes. Goethe wrote in the *Farbenlehre*, "Everything alive is not a singular but a plural. The German has for the complex that constitutes the living actuality of a being the word 'Gestalt.' " Restating Goethe in his own language, Whitehead offers us most welcome news. If we can believe him, imagination in our own era is not dead, as we would have assumed—judging solely by the display of murderous abstractions around us and from our own visits to Bergamo. It can be trained, awakened as memory in the manner Plato [35] understood it: "Seeing the beauty here below, and having a reminiscence of the true." It can be trained until it reaches the disinterested height where everything, factories and boundary disputes included, can become "Gestalt" in the Goethean sense.

Here science becomes intellectual salvation, an art. To create "vivid values" one might call a twice-born science, a science which becomes, for the sake of truth, consciously impractical. It is like a picture of a pretty girl for a magazine cover or advertisement—practical, as an auspicious increase of sales figures will soon indicate, but in order to become truth the symbol, abstracted in the interest of a social purpose, has to be reborn. The obviously shapely girl whose boundaries are the boundaries of the signboard has to become the kind of impersonal, disinterested, involved, and boundless accumulation of situations and ages which boarded Walter Pater's imagination for a memorable cruise around the rocks and enigmas of the Mona Lisa.[36] This is neither popular nor easy—but the popular and easy moves the market, not the cosmos.

I remember how horrified a daughter of a distinguished physicist was when her father's discovery acquired sudden unexpected renown because it was the promise of a great popular invention. He had tried, the daughter informed me, to think along the lines of the Architect of the Universe, to establish in the medieval sense the *adaequatio rei et intellectus*, to use matter as a proof for the consistency of the spirit. "Now he is spoken of as an inventor, as if it had been his intention to add to the noise of society."

It will be pointed out that it makes no difference whether a fact is socially useful or not; in order to make sense at all it has to be grasped from the point of view of the Architect of the Universe, from the point of view of objective law. The much decried mechanics of civilization are therefore an objectivation of the spirit, in the sense in which Sir James Jeans[37] contends that the thoughts of a mathematician coincide with the thoughts of the Architect of the Universe, because the Architect of the Universe is a mathematician. But the story of the physicist's daughter should make the difference between an objectivation of the spirit in an interested and a disinterested sense quite clear: in the first instance not the total fact, but the utilizable fact, is sought for; in the second instance not man's insatiable and illusory hunger for "progress" is back of the procedure, but faith that to translate the mystery of things into symbols from an ever more profound viewpoint, that to retreat "ever deeper into the recesses of the total fact," will bring human restlessness ultimately to rest in an enlarged consciousness.[38]

Against the disrupting practicality of the surface mind we are positing not the anarchy of Nature and the anarchy of the Spirit, but the Goethean "Gestalt"—like Time a moving image of Eternity, and indeed, like the Mona Lisa, the essence of Duration. If the European bourgeoisie had not committed the most un-Goethean and un-European sin of treating science and education well-nigh exclusively as a tool for the servile, or mechanical, arts, and if it had not relegated the liberal arts, the "theory" in the Aristotelean sense, to the remotest corner of decorative insignificance, the phenomenon Hitler would have been impossible. The "hereditary disposition of sensibility" would not have tolerated it. But the "hereditary disposition of sensibility" had been ruthlessly destroyed by the interested empiricism of European education. Of course it is possible to argue that Hitlerism, like Marxism, is the organized vulgarity of the uninitiated masses. The bourgeoisie, however, have failed to weave the spell which would have made an initiation into the life of the spirit and its formative power appear worthwhile in the eyes of the masses. The masses wanted what to all appearances the bourgeois had and enjoyed having: not wisdom, but material advantages. The bourgeois made a spiritual evaluation of poverty on Franciscan lines impossible.

Paradoxically, what science means—not as handmaid of the servile arts but on the level of art and religion as "intellectual salvation," as "growth of meaning," as a creative rebirth which, in Bertrand Russell's phrase, comforts like the beatific vision [39]—has been formulated in terms of rare felicity in Soviet Russia. Ivanov and Gershenson lived in Moscow in two opposite corners of the same room in 1920. Undaunted by the uncomfortable fact of their crowded quarters, they practised intellectual salvation by sending each other comments in time and out of time over the diagonal of their apartment—Gershenson a prophet of *tabula rasa*, Ivanov a prophet of the soul made pregnant by venerable historical antecedents. "To me culture is a ladder of Eros and a hierarchy of reverences." Culture, so far as it expresses merely man, is oppressive; but so far as it bears witness to the liberty which is at the core of autonomous creation, it gives us wings. It depends on our faith in the Absolute, independent from culture, whether we have inward liberty, liberty that is the essence of Life, or whether we have inward servitude.

In 1932, just before Hitler came to power, the German Ernst Robert Curtius made these and other thoughts of Ivanov the centre of a most eloquent pamphlet significantly called *German Spirit in Peril*.[40] He employed Ivanov's words in order to remind his compatriots that a community is ultimately judged by the quality of spiritual initiation which it is able to offer to its members.

The destruction of Europe is the logical consequence of the pernicious folly of leaving untrained the "memory" which, Ivanov says, is a dynamic principle, the principle that enables us to renew in ourselves the initiations of our ancestors. The Occident was a shoe factory before it became a cemetery. But the Platonic, Confucian, and Thomistic community was, in

# BIRTH AND DEATH OF THE SPIRIT 99

the words of Ivanov, an initiation. What loyalty can we have for a community which practises the abolition of the soul?

One of the best parables of a community fulfilling its ideal part I have found in a little-known passage in Goethe's *Sprueche in Prosa:* "In a badly built town the citizen is exiled into the wilderness of a sinister disposition." But then Goethe introduces Orpheus himself as architect of an ideal city: "Stones, enthusiastically advancing, grew into shape in accordance with the best rules of the craft, and rhythmically ranged themselves in layers and walls.... The sounds vanish, the harmony persists. The inhabitants of such a city move and act between eternal melodies; the spirit cannot sink, activity cannot grow dull; the eye takes over function and duty of the ear, and the citizens, on the most undistinguished day, are transported into an ideal disposition; without reflection, without asking for the reason, they participate in the highest moral and religious delights...."

To return to Whitehead. Intuition makes matter join the procession of values which "arise from the cumulation, in some sense, of the brooding presence of the Whole onto its various parts." [41] These values, to interpret this passage for our argument, are rooted in warm maternal Eternity and refuse to make the unfeeling millstones of civilization turn, as superficial motives do.

But this is precisely what elicits from Wyndham Lewis a memorable outburst. Because this outburst characterizes the standpoint of contemporary society, struggling as it is against the influx of the Whole, we cite it here. Attacking Whitehead and Samuel Alexander, Lewis exclaims: [42] "So these philosophers are busy disintegrating for us our public material paradise, and propose to give us in exchange the dark and feverish confusion of their 'mental' truth, no longer confined to the units of the organic world but released into everything." "The researches," he says, "of the man of science into the laws of matter had proverbially valuable results. He treated this matter of his as essentially a system of effects, and entirely left out of count all questions of a cause. Such a man-of-science, if rather a dry stick, was a respectable figure who did no direct harm to anybody and was able, even to do the richer members of the community—manufacturers, steamship owners, armament makers and so forth—a great deal of good. They formed a very high opinion of science and of 'matter': and by means of their organs of publicity taught everybody else to value science highly, for the power it gave a ruling caste over its fellow-men (interpreted in the science tract or the daily paper as 'man's power over nature'). These activities continue as before."

If we understand Lewis rightly, science seems no longer content with furnishing the middle class the weapons which reduce the total and intangible aspect of existence into tangible and profitable segments: "It has of late the ambition to see beyond the utilitarian façade right into the eyes of Truth." It has introduced an absolute into the nature beneath its control. Whitehead's or Alexander's "organic" nature is an "absolute."

This quotation may not teach us much about Whitehead or Alexander or the Absolute; but it reflects, in a form whose facetiousness Wyndham Lewis himself may explain, the great argument beneath the outward struggle of our time: the battle between two realities, two sciences, two truths—intellect which is directly useful to man, and a synthetic disposition, the "pneuma" which is absolute and useless; one which makes "manufacturers, steamship owners, armament makers and so forth" happy, and the other which makes them unhappy because it is the invention of eccentrics and of wayward characters who dwell in the wilderness and eat locusts.

I see an explanation for the tragic and fatal, the disastrous German maladjustment and non-conformism, an explanation which I pass on to the re-educators, in the fact that to be maladjusted in the machine age was bound to become, for a certain mentality to which I myself was not a stranger, almost a title of intellectual nobility. It was like taking orders in the brotherhood of the Absolute, or being admitted into the knighthood of the Spirit. To cease making the "richer members of the community" happy was almost synonymous with being initiated into the mysteries of the Universe. We are going to discuss this in the next chapter. Here it remains to be said that one gigantic question mark threw its shadow over the anti-bourgeois crusade for the liberation of the forgotten Original in our lives: the philosophy of Oswald Spengler.

According to Spengler, anti-bourgeois crusades are fights against windmills—not because Spengler is fond of the bourgeois, quite the opposite, but because the bourgeois is the genuine expression of our age. But, says Spengler, we have no choice but to accept the fact in all its ugliness. Our own contribution should be to make that ugliness overwhelming until it assumes the character of conscious expression of an inevitable state of mind. Goethe's, Whitehead's, Schopenhauer's, and Bergson's contemplative thinking, the capacity of meeting, when entering the everyday scene, the idea rather than the fact of the milkman and the bus is, according to Spengler, a kind of Grace which we have irredeemably lost, as Adam and Eve lost paradise, and for the same reason: Adam and Eve lost paradise because they learned to "know" what they should have been content to "live." But unlike Adam and Eve, we lost paradisiac support not through any individual sin of our own, but because we had the misfortune to be born into a time which, grown old and even senile, excludes a naïve communion with the organic power of the Whole. We know, indeed, not because we ate the forbidden fruit, but because we cannot help knowing. That we are cut off with our whole generation from the sources of Being is the characteristic of our age.

Our knowledge is a substitute for Being, just as civilization is a substitute for intuition. You cannot have your cake and eat it. Either you are an instrument in a great orchestra conducted by the creative energy, the flute on which the god Krishna plays, and then you have to submit your ego to the style dictates of "Culture"; or you sever your ties with the formative principle which presides over your cultural entelechy, and rely on the greed of your emancipated ego, like the rest of society: but then you are just a wheel that performs a quantity of meaningless rotations in the nerve-wrecking routine of civilization.

Not this antithesis, however, separates Spengler from Whitehead and Bergson, but the proposition that the Western world is inevitably the prisoner of civilization in the twentieth century. Both Spengler and Whitehead worship "Gestalt"; but Spengler condemns modern man as constitutionally incapable of "Gestalt." A dangerous thought if ever there was one, because by putting the man of the twentieth century in the "winter" of a certain morphological year which started about A.D. 1000, he denies him the activities of all other seasons, including the cultivation of autumnal wisdom which was the inwardly-directed activity of eighteenth-century Goethe—an activity by which "the pull of the phenomenal world is diminished and the mind is placed at the disposal of the subconscious powers."

This patient self-effacement out of loyalty to the deeper self, this precious method of diminishing the noise of the market by the noisy claims of the top mind, and eventually of adding a new intuition to the shrine of past intuitions—Whitehead permits the entertainment of such hopes, but Spengler denies them. So far as Western man is concerned, there is no "deeper self" left. To dig for it is sheer waste of time.

"I am teaching here," writes Spengler in the introduction to the *Decline of the West*,[43] "that one must see in Imperialism the typical symbol of a late epoch. Imperialism is pure civilization. In this phenomenon the destiny of the Occident is irrevocably set. A man of cultural epochs turns his energy inwards, a man of civilized epochs outwards. That is why I see in Cecil Rhodes the first man of a new era. He represents the political style of a still distant, occidental, Germanic, specifically German future. His saying 'Extension is everything' sums up in this Napoleonic terseness the typical tendency of each mature civilization. That applies to Romans, Arabs, Chinese. No choice is possible. Not even the conscious will of the individual or of classes and peoples can here decide. The expansive tendency is a fatum, something demoniac and immense which seizes the late man of the metropolitan era, which enslaves and consumes him whether he likes it or not, whether he knows it or not. Life is the realization of possibilities, and for intellectual man only extensive possibilities exist."

Space, then, and expansion into space, is our destiny, if we believe Spengler. Civilization, dynamic and will-obsessed, is our incurable disease, our horribly active senility which finds its deadly climax and realization in the symbol of late epochs, imperialism. Spengler peoples an unsympathetic and unresponsive world with monologues of will which drive their lethal weapons against each other until the strongest will imposes the peace of the cemetery upon the unhappy globe. This, crudely simplified, is the lesson Spengler teaches. He picks Rhodes as the exemplary man of our time because he is "Roman": divorced from meaning, ethos, and tradition, the will-to-power sets into motion "coldest, most abstract measures." Success becomes a problem of engineering. In abysmal solitude the modern Caesars plough through the winter of time; compared to them, Alexander and Napoleon were still invested with the last glow of feeling. Intellectual energy is possible in our time, but not the creative energy which we associate with the life of the spirit.

It is difficult to exaggerate the importance of Spengler's writings in Europe, especially, of course, in Germany. Spengler turned his knowledge of Goethe against Goethe. We are born with an un-Goethean face and must honor our physiognomy by living up to its implications. It is as if a man with a murderous physiognomy should feel in duty bound to commit a murder. Like Marx and Nietzsche, Spengler was angered by the so-called idealism in which the selfhood of the bourgeois was wrapping itself, and he felt a compelling urge to answer complacency with a statement of his resentment. The effect of his voluminous and hypnotizing diatribe was enormous. I still feel it in all my bones—my surroundings, this lying, empty, abstract, and yet painfully normal façade of the machine age, had suddenly acquired for the first time, through Spengler, the status of a thought. This gloomy world of success philosophy in its utter unrelatedness came once more antithetically to life, if only as a figure of death. Caliban saw his ugliness in a mirror, and instead of howling, rejoiced, because ugliness was his destiny. This was 1920. A fateful start for the long armistice between two world wars.

To sum up: Either Whitehead and the Bergsoneans are right, either it is possible to work towards the Whole, and the Whole will work towards you, will emancipate you from the particular, will graft you upon its spontaneity, will make you complete, a microcosm, trailing clouds of "Gestalten"; or if completeness is denied, as Spengler and a whole era deny it, civilization, a man-made centipede, multiplying its limbs and digging for food, inevitably runs into space. If you then try to stop it, likely as not it will forget which foot to move first, and lift the wrong one. The logical position to take under these circumstances is: never stop civilization. Even if it is a mistake, it is a mistake that works, that raises cities, that fires the night sky with the reflex of the Great White Way, that shakes the earth with drums of steel and clarions of steam; it is a wonderful and gigantic mistake, a human and humanistic and anthropocentric mistake. If the Spirit of the Whole sends us to hell for it, it is worth it.

# CHAPTER III

# THE REVIVAL OF THE SPIRIT FAILS

> *Half a fool's kingdom, far from*
> *men who sow and reap,*
> *All their days, vanity....*
>
> —Ernest Dowson,
> *To One in Bedlam*

A LITTLE EARLIER I SAID, WITH A PERSONAL TWIST which I hope will be forgiven, that I was not a total stranger to an attitude of non-conformism in a bourgeois world which worships time as the equivalent of money and despises time as the equivalent of wisdom. I also said that one should be careful not to ascribe victory in the second world war to the principles of plutocracy or communism, Hitler's avowed pet hatreds, but to a higher definition of life's meaning. Furthermore I suggested that one of the main purposes of this book is to show why those who believe that a higher definition of life's meaning has little to do with a specific economic environment should not therefore be called partners of Hitler, who in his horribly popular manner said something like this.

It is true that Hitler attacked plutocracy and communism, which are not exactly praised in this book either; but I want to make it quite clear in the present and the following chapter that this similarity is purely coincidental. I wonder why intelligent people like Ezra Pound, Henri de Montherlant, and others who mingled their gypsy voices with the voices of gangsters in the denunciation of the modern world, did not see the issue more clearly. One can criticize the social agent of the machine age, the middle class, because it hinders a higher definition of life's meaning and therefore blocks the realization of the inner meaning of the machine, namely detachment from drudgery and peace for the sake of contemplation. But Hitler's propaganda apparatus criticized the middle class from the opposite angle: his attacks were caused by his contempt for what from his point of view were reactionary features of middle-class rule—impractical and, to Hitler, hypocritical decencies. These Victorian remnants and *gemuetlichen* clichés had been condemned to death in Spengler's catalogue of doom, and therefore, in the eyes of the Nazis, had no right any longer to bother the clever satanism of the New Order. Not the secular habits of the bourgeoisie, not the cold mechanical planning and obsession with quantities, were objectionable to the Nazis. No, wrong in their eyes were the inhibitions of the correct burgher, which kept alive in the modern ice age the flowers of a warmer climate of the heart—Christian inhibitions which the age of progress had not been able to dissolve but which the nihilists were out to kill.

The meaning of this our time, according to Spengler, is meaninglessness, and anything that softened the impact of this knowledge stood in the way of Hitler's diabolism. We shall go into that in the next chapter. Here I feel it would not be too much out of place if I explain how I happened to dissociate myself from this nihilism. So far I have only indicated that I walked through the paraphernalia of the European scene, Bergamo, for instance, with no memories within me responding to the memories which the Great Tradition had stored up. I have also indicated that Spengler's categorical imperative addressed to mechanized souls like myself, and ordering us to live out the mechanism in our soul—that Spengler's gospel of meaninglessness offered me the first true meaning I had discovered in life. But one day the manna fell from heaven, and I discovered a second true meaning. A visit to the Cathedral of Chartres was the occasion. It was during this visit that I was seized by the most profound transport I have ever felt. The fact that I was emotionally a mummy was shattered in a gale of the Spirit "which bloweth as it listeth" and that dilated and purged all my clotted cells. Everybody should have his Bethel to which he can turn, as the Mohammedans turn to Mecca; my Bethel and my Mecca, the thought of which is enough to renew in me the dimension I once felt, is Chartres. It is the image of unattached Spirit—it is more than an image, it is its reality.

If I see the facts of our century with the eyes of this experience, everything is solved. There are the quantities, there are the shallow waters of consciousness, complacency, and resentment which divide the world into exclusiveness of privilege and exclusiveness of hate, there are the particularized and spatialized objects and moods which clash if the motors that move them operate from the surface. Yet, the moment I enter this Inferno with the spirit which Chartres has the unique gift to invoke, even ugliness, projected on a higher plane, becomes the note in a song.

The Cathedral of Chartres is a plain fact that signifies to those who have eyes to see the high-water mark to which the flood of European consciousness once rose. From this we should deduce first the need for "eyes to see," second that we should be able, in our own special circumstances, to mold the material under our hands as perfectly as the anonymous people of Chartres were able to do eight hundred years ago. Modernism is not a chronological fact, or a fact of material progress, but a fact whose evaluation depends on the evidence whether our chronological and material progress has enabled us to reach the high-water mark of consciousness earlier generations have set, and more important, whether we can advance beyond it.

If, then, ages and nations compete for the advancement of the inner unity of life in our consciousness, Chartres, to me, is the most progressive document on this globe. Here is the spot where the world genius, the *élan vital*, thirsting for freedom, threw his golden spear far ahead into the *mêlée* of history, thus marking to the generations that were to follow the territory they ought to conquer. "All the steam in the world could not, like the Virgin, build Chartres," wrote Henry Adams. The Virgin, to a non-theological mind like mine, is the maternal Universe, the divine impetus which works in the stuff of life towards its liberation, and whose liberation is accomplished every time our individual shell bursts, and our immortal core steps out into the open, awakened to its universal Oneness, using our limbs and features merely as the inconsequential garment of the moment. This is what has happened in Chartres.

The whole community was penetrated with quality and thus was "basically equal" in the transcendental sense, which gives equality its title of nobility. Not only prince and peasant dragged the stones to the site, as a famous contemporary letter tells us, but we have the evidence before us in stone and glass that prince as well as peasant, settled burgher as well as unsettled beggar, were "one" in sustaining with their enthusiasm those who handled the material. The grocer around the corner and the butcher from across the street were the "equals" of Aeschylus, St. John, Shakespeare, and Beethoven. If you do not believe me, go and see how much grace, luxury, and perfection flowed from the hands of the common man in Chartres.

The experience of Chartres taught me two distinct lessons: first, a new definition of democracy, and second, the conviction that Spengler's winter tale of the soul, the actuality of steam and the inactuality of the Virgin, was wrong. I shall treat these two points one after another.

I confess that I used to be a good European and a bad American, in the sense that I was convinced that life ceased to be worth living with the advent of democracy in Europe. Without any help from Spengler I had found out that democracy in Europe signified the victory of the filling-station operator, who takes his business seriously, over the occidental counterparts of Prince Arjuna, who was taught by a god to take seriously only the ennobling of his functions by detachment. To the extent to which imagination in Europe was submerged in the prose of the nineteenth century and the elite withered because society preferred the dumb, amorphous coral reefs of success to a beautiful and intelligent doubt in the significance of society's enterprise—to this extent I mourned the cheapening of Europe's once mighty spells. From this point of view there seemed nothing wicked in the traditional European distrust of democracy and the mechanics of freedom, provided only that this distrust was provoked and conditioned by another and more significant freedom: *freedom from the inconsequential.* The progressive removal of perspective from the centre of European affairs and the progressive substitution in its place of the friction of senselessly agitated social atoms could only end in what William Morris called, with reference to Bellamy, "a horrible cockney's dream of the millennium."

Baudelaire found the last man worthy of his name among

the dandies—"representatives of an urge to combat and to destroy the trivial." In the period of transition when democracy has not yet won entirely, and aristocracy is not yet totally dead, the dandies form a new aristocracy, the last, based "on the celestial gifts which work and money cannot convey." "Dandyism" is a "setting sun," superb, without warmth and full of melancholy. "Alas, the mounting deluge of democracy," says Baudelaire, "invading and levelling everything, is about to drown these last envoys from the province of human hauteur." [1]

Compared to this futile, harmless snobbery, Napoleon-worship proved a more effective challenge to the defeats the progressive bourgeois inflicted on the spirit for the sake of comfort. Already Victor Hugo—playing liberty's martyr in the face of Napoleon III's gaslighted and stucco-adorned essay in fascism that was based on the approval of the masses—cried in the dramatic silence of his exile: "Can you picture to yourself a man voluntarily blind? This terrible thing exists. There are willing slaves—there is a smile in irons." And yet, he should have known the answer. He himself, in the French Chamber in the days of Louis Philippe, had evoked the awful ghost of the first Napoleon that it might drive the petty ghosts of ennui, meanness, and sordidness from the temple of France. "I am tempted to say to the Chamber, to the press and to all France: Let us speak of the Emperor, it will do us good."

All through the nineteenth century and up to the first world war, the Napoleonic saga was the most powerful myth encountered by the swelling boa constrictor of European ennui. It not only played a role in a positive sense, as a source of a *frisson*, but also negatively it provided the prime occasion to *épater le bourgeois*. If you cannot be creative, at least be demoniac. If you approach the phenomenon Napoleon from the point of view of the aristocrat, as Chateaubriand did in the *Mémoires d'Outre-Tombe* and Tolstoi in *War and Peace*, the Emperor becomes a parvenu. But if you compare him with the philistine, as did most German apostles of the Corsican, like Goethe, Heine, and Nietzsche, the Bonapartian epic becomes "music which extinguishes civilization." When Heine, as a boy, saw the Emperor ride through the Hofgarten in Duesseldorf, he was particularly impressed that the little man with his three-cornered hat calmly dared to use the main alley where horseback riding was strictly prohibited under threat of a fine of five thalers. In his prose essay *Italy* Heine, the very leftist Heine, says in so many words that though the aristocrats made war against Napoleon, the great man made war not against aristocrats, whom he loved and of whom he was one, but against the philistines.

When a boy in Germany wanted to anger the middle class in whose midst he grew up and whose cautious moves shelved life as if it were another pot of jam, he professed admiration for Napoleon. Though far from having acquired either wife or children, he sang, "Was schert mich Weib, was schert mich Kind," and regretted that it was too late to enroll against clichés under the banner of a tyranny which looked like spontaneity. To illustrate with Heine once more: In the *Buch Le Grand* he made St. Helena into a Golgotha and the mediocre English governor Sir Hudson Lowe into the Pontius Pilate of the nineteenth century, who condemned to death the last spark of imagination which was threatening to disturb the great sound sleep of materialism.

"With Napoleon only Earth and Water count," said Goethe, who preferred Earth and Water to the bourgeois notion of nationalism. Napoleon was only a characteristic incident in the life of Goethe, his rendezvous with the "daemon," with a rather impure "actus purus" through which destiny seemed to speak for once its own direct if terrifying language. It was the element, the per se, which attracted Goethe to Napoleon, the Earth and Water, their catastrophes and fertilities rolled into one. Goethe had a way of expressing his intimacy with the elements in that happy and circumstantial emanation from the Ultimate that, parallel to Earth and Water, reaches our perception as language, melody, rhythm, wisdom, love, and metaphor.

And now, in Chartres, I was confronted with grocers and butchers who had been truly elite; who had been elemental like Napoleon, yet, better than Napoleon, had not expressed their fundamental nature in catastrophes but had unfolded it fastidiously with Goethean fullness and grace by means of an enormous monument which it took a century to build; and who even better than Goethe, with angelic skill, had hauled the celestial tiers filled with witnesses and martyrs down to earth because this was the company, the atmosphere, and the ferment in which they felt at home. In Chartres, therefore, I saw the only possible answer to the modern predicament: The defeat of quality by quantity, of spontaneity by organization, can be reversed if two conditions which existed in the Middle Ages are fulfilled, if people consider the "therapeutics of the soul" the real object of their existence, and if Time is given an opportunity to exercise its power so that the moments of the inward pilgrimage, the memories, inspirations, colors, thunders, and melodies of the ascent toward the Absolute can be gathered into a synthesis and shaped into an expression. Here again we have "kairos"—the time that works toward, and contains, fulfillment; the definite Christian counterpart to Bergson's indefinite duration. Through immersion in the processes and intuitions of creative time the dry twig of quantity will blossom into quality, and the revolving masses will pause to see "books in the running brooks, sermons in stones and good in everything"—this at least is what my own revolving ego saw in a flash when standing bareheaded before the miracle of Chartres.

The second lesson that Chartres taught me is this: The curtain that fell over a meaningful human history can rise again any time, even without Spengler's permission. The principle of history is not the fatalistic living out of morphological cycles, with all your behaviour mapped out for you by the season into which you are born; it is a pendulum, with every statement breeding its contradiction, every positive its negative, every condition the unconditioned. The empire of externalized fact, of militant particulars, of clashing sections, and fertile voids was crumbling—I saw it clearly that day in Chartres. Its opposite, the inward act, was raising its head. And I am not afraid to say that I believed that the swing of the pendulum back from space to time, from organization to organism, and from intellect to wisdom would ultimately be achieved with the help of a substantial contribution on the part of Germany.

Here is the reason why an observer, seven years before Hitler, could misjudge the swing of the pendulum: There had been a fall of the Spirit, but after 1900 a secret counter current had set in; the harshness of the air began to be softened at places; the anatomy of modern man slowly lost in certain instances its angular and pedestrian features; innumerable windows were opened; the globe became again a meeting place and exchange of visitors and notions which had travelled over individual roads to a common universality. The pendulum seemed to swing back. I shall give a catalogue of the symptoms later.

In many respects the time during the 1920's is like the Indian summer of 1800, of the idealistic-romantic effervescence whose representative *summa* was the work of Goethe. The effervescence about 1800 was by no means a purely German phenomenon. It was occidental. But it seized Germany and Austria with memorable fervor and thoroughness, it became a passion, an obsession—or rather, it became an element outside of which the disciple of the Logos could not exist. Gregory of Nyssa, who lived in the fourth century, tells us that the Byzantium of his time surrendered so madly to spiritual excitement that when he wanted a loaf of bread people informed him that the Son is inferior to the Father, and when he inquired whether the bath were ready, he was invited to discuss the possibility that the Son was made of nothing.

Madame de Staël noticed something similar in the Germany of her day; she was amazed to see common laborers, bricklayers, and stonecutters, seek rest from their exertions with highbrow literature in their hand. "Saxony is of profound tranquillity; occasionally there is some noise about some ideas, but nobody thinks to apply them in real life. It looks as if thinking and acting have nothing to do with each other, and as if Truth, with the Germans, is like the statue of Hermes which has neither hands to hold nor feet to advance. There is however nothing so much worthy of our respect as these conquests of the imagination, which keep people occupied who live in isolation, who have no money, no power, and who are united amongst themselves only by the cult of the idea."

Here we have the proper elevation—people without power and without money, but fully and splendidly occupied by an idea. Germany, "ces Indes de l'Europe," contented herself with conquests of the imagination. Germany did not move because it was "petrified by the spell of the Infinite." Like the hero and heroine in *Axel's Castle*, and in truly Albigensian fashion, the romanticists began to despise an ideal the moment it was soiled and spoiled by realization. They aspired to live, like the Rishis in India, permanently on the level of profundity; they hunted the butterfly Intuition in groves which their descendants were to cut down for the sake of efficiency. Jean Paul considered it an "impropriety" to desire both "the immortal bouquets of fantasy and the thin flowers of earthly happiness": "If down here the poem should become actuality, and our pastoral a sheep pen, and each dream a real day, this would never fulfill our wishes, it would only add to them; the higher reality would give birth to a higher poetry, in Arcady we would yearn for Utopia...."

At the time of Goethe's death, the international prestige of the German "Geist" for turning the silver of the particular into the gold of the universal had reached its peak. In Russia young men associated with Alexander Herzen, Belinsky, and Pushkin embraced each other with the name of Schiller on their lips, while in Massachusetts bold spirits called themselves transcendentalists in homage to Kant, and Margaret Fuller collected data for her admirable essay on Goethe. Victor Hugo was to write, in his *Shakespeare*, the most resounding apostrophe ever conceived in appraisal, and one might as well say in praise, of Germany, "India of the West." The Frenchman Edgar Quinet moved happily with God- and poetry-inspired pundits, the Arnims, Creuzers, Brentanos, Goerres, in the polyphonic woods of Heidelberg. Yet it was Quinet who for the first time sounded the alarm in a famous article which appeared in 1831 in the *Revue des Deux Mondes*. "What we are witnessing today in Germany is a fall of the spirit. The heavenly Jerusalem is crashing into the abyss. No hand can arrest her doom." [2]

Quinet mysteriously foresaw the growing power of Prussia, a rising continent of the will which would make Germany great and the Germans small. However, to blame Prussia for the intellectual and artistic collapse of Germany after 1871 is hardly to the point. The German middle class wanted to be made small, it wanted to eat its thickly-buttered bread in a setting of selfhood and short range effects which was not typical for the Prussian style. Prussia, before it was invaded by the triumphant bourgeois, was a style, a responsibility. It was originally a task which, taken all in all, implied a long view and an idea.

Even justifiable prejudice cannot deny that in the unattractive, sandy plains of North Germany Prussia had planted a "Gestalt" which looked distressingly like duty and hardly Mozartian; yet patience and abnegation can endear Cinderella to first-rate philosophers like Kant, Fichte, and Hegel. How often did I compare the Wilhelmstrasse, whose style, reflecting ethos instead of relaxation, reminded one of American puritanism, with the Kurfuerstendamm, the *via triumphalis* of greenest success; how often did I wonder what philosopher the real estate agents who built these empty *fortissimi* in Berlin Westend could quote in defense of their doings. Even Epicurus would have thrown up his arms. The "Gestalt" Prussia, which the extraordinary will power of Bismarck endangered as he served it, became a threat to the world only when it was dissolved in the German tidal wave Bismarck had unwittingly unloosed. Its secret virtue was thrown on the market, its discipline became a practical credo, a meaningless, directionless experimenting with the technique of success. The bourgeois, eager to be defeated spiritually, found his apotheosis in William II. The pendulum had swung all the way from the inward to the outward pole.

I said in the second chapter that to be maladjusted in the machine age amounted, for a certain mentality in Germany, almost to a title of intellectual nobility. Ever since Nietzsche uttered his great cry that rolled from the lofty Thebaid of the Alps, the crystalline loneliness of the Engadine, down into the stuffy overcrowded plains of a Europe that bred not only reptiles, but dinosaurs—ever since 1900, some crazy and fantastic revolt against the abject capitulation of the German middle class before the temptations of the power age was due. It was a prophecy turned backwards, the rescuing of fairy-tale spontaneity, of "Stille Nacht" innocence, but also of mightier accents which would end the bondage of the ego, and turn man into an instrument of the Whole. Surrounded by an angelic host in stone, I had interpreted in Chartres these stirrings as a possible movement of our whole century towards the point where mass and elite shall meet again. I am now leaving my stand in front of the adorable cathedral in order to examine whether the swing of the pendulum back from the outward to the inward pole which I hopefully foresaw in the 1920's was real enough to offer a new soul.

## REVIVAL OF THE SPIRIT FAILS

Let me say first that a clever re-educator would ally himself with any tendency which honors the profoundly impractical above the unprofoundly practical. A clever re-educator would prefer this kind of non-conformism to the two unsuccessful essays in conformism on the part of Germany—I mean the two world wars in which Germany tried to surpass the cleverness of the world not with otherworldliness, but with an unfettered superlative of worldliness. A good and wise re-educator would seek out the dumb Michel, the symbol of the impractical stargazer, a Sir Galahad on the verge of failure. A Hitler will never understand that attachment, and even love, for Germany can be bound up with the existence of this almost providential failure in the heart of the bulky, hard, oppressive German fact. A Hitler always thinks in terms of success. But a wise re-educator would look for the wings which the albatross has folded in the prison of a cheap delusion. He would ally himself with the odd and only partly rewarded manoeuvres by which the Germans tried, against the sign of the time, to catch the paradise bird of a total world view—which, when they thought they had caught it, was consumed by a monster, the bastard totality of Hitler.[3]

But this tendency of the German to evaporate after he has become so heavy that the globe fairly quakes under his foot will hardly be encouraged. Both the materialistic perversion of the elemental by Hitler and the anachronistic pursuits on the part of the dumb Michel are unpopular. No other alternative will be offered but the prison of reason [4]—which breeds reptiles.

A few years ago a book appeared here which contained valuable material with respect to German basic non-conformism: Aurel Kolnai, *The War against the West*.[5] Not all the schemes Kolnai exposes in his book are innocent, but many are; many are moulds conceived in the hope that the dried-up Ganges of imagination might be induced to flow into them again. "Gestalt," writes Kolnai, "that war-cry of modern German thought!" Is the statement that society once upon a time reflected, as "Gestalt," the formative processes of life—is this a declaration of war against the West? Wyndham Lewis was able to unearth quite a few people in the West, and there are many more, who felt that the powers of the Universe were needed to supplement the sterility of the machine. It is calumny to assert that the war against the West is the war of the Absolute, and the war of the West the war against the Absolute. Hitler conceived the Absolute as the image of his resentment, but a form, a "Gestalt" that is the focus of the Absolute, implies disinterestedness and distance. Form means an expression in actuality that somebody, or a whole people, or a whole time, has reached a secret understanding with a higher actuality, a Whole or Completeness. Creativeness is effectively bearing witness that the ascent from relationship to relationship, the "Growth of Meaning," has begun.

If it is true, as one reads in newspapers, that the United Nations "do not make war against German music," re-educators should distinguish better than Kolnai and Wyndham Lewis between motives and goals of the different brands which grace or disgrace the quaint collection of German and European irrationalisms. One cannot merely take law and reason and call it plus, and then turn against those who feel that law and reason "do not change the disposition of the heart," and call such a school of thought minus. The tree is known by its fruit. The "value blindness" of the modern world produced "hollow men." Because people felt that law and reason should do more than "do the richer members of the community a great deal of good," because they felt that the mystery of existence was not adequately expressed by this particular use of law and reason, they began to look behind law and reason. This "looking behind law and reason" without thought of worldly success was, roughly speaking, the theme of the expressionistic Germany which slowly emerged after 1900; it was the dance of the paradise bird which was killed by Hitler for the sake of worldly success. This at least is my thesis.

The expressionistic Germany, an attempt to revive the Weimar component of the German system in the bewildering environment of the machine age, was both exceedingly pagan and exceedingly religious—religious in an undogmatic, mystic, inspirational sense; and the experimental approaches to salvation, tried frantically by an uprooted generation outside the exigencies of the machine age, make a queer story.

The attempt to give "un sense nouveau aux mots de la tribu," to yearn for the wonder-working region of synthesis, to define existence by new co-ordinates which originated in the higher mathematics of the heart, seemed the only revolution that really counted in our time, the only revolution worthy of Albigensians who missed the Pythian afflatus. It all started with a challenge of the pretences of Wilhelminian society. William II, around whom the bourgeoisie crowded in breathless adulation, preferred to gild the empty progress of his reign with showmanship rather than to visit once the huge, crammed, bedbug-ridden, proletarian quarter of East Berlin, though his palace was situated right on the edge of it. Callousness was in the best laissez-faire tradition, but it was a sin from the point of view of the patriarchal tradition, and it might amuse the reader to know that there were people in Germany who attributed the pronounced bourgeois traits in Wilhelm's character to his English mother. Here it is enough to repeat that the air of the Wilhelminian era was heavily scented with melodramatic pretences which rested on such overwhelming evidence of German prowess as alarm clocks, aniline dyes, and newfangled machines of war.

But impatience with this almost idiotic fertility of pretences had grown steadily since Nietzsche, and especially since the disaster of 1918 started a crusade for more genuine bases of contentment, a crusade recruited from all possible disgruntled and disappointed allegiances surviving in the unbalanced country. Already before 1918 enough literary and artistic thunder and lightning had gathered to make anybody but the bourgeois shake; he, however, entrenched behind his colossal "buffets" weighed down by bulging cups, plates, ewers, and saltcellars feigned monumental indifference. Frivolous manifestations of intangible significance, so far as they entered his ken, filled him with contempt. Spengler's book appeared in 1917, and was directed of course against the stifling optimism of the Wilhelminian era. In the same year Rudolf Otto's *Idea of the Holy* was published, and religion ceased to be a textbook for the theological faculty and a bogeyman for naughty children. The outlawed province of man's introverted nature found unexpected champions in the philosophers of the subconscious. Ancient spells of Asia and Africa, prostrated continents which served as happy hunting grounds for the waking consciousness of Western chemists and entrepreneurs, were suddenly understood in Berlin and Munich; novel interpretations of China, India, and Egypt were traded; stars, flowers, and romanticism were reborn; Franz Marc painted with Master Eckhart and Jacob Boehme in his heart. The German stage became exciting and cosmopolitan, if only to serve as an antidote to a society which was dull, narrow, and nationalistic. While patriotic orators and newspapers played up one version of human possibilities, the importance of being successful, Nijinsky leaped through the twenty stories of bourgeois success into the freedom of a tremendous gesture. He was followed by a cloud of dancing Germans whose earnestness introduced an element of self-flagellation into their attempts to reach freedom through rhythm.

Quite a while before, Hauptmann had already thrown open the gates of the poor man's ghetto with his *Weber*, and had written *Emanuel Quint*, the common man made into Christ; Kaethe Kollwitz sketched the carmagnoles of slum dwellers; and Stefan George made his Rhenish vineyard the starting point for a solemn exodus from the prose age into the blue recesses of the ideal world theatre. Stefan George and the Germanic-Romanic chorus by which he was surrounded lifted themselves through style, the *Kraft des schoenen Lebens*, into the neighbourhood of a pure inspiration. Daeubler hurled on the market three fat volumes of an azure song in honor of the Ararat and the aurora borealis. Munich acquired the reputation of harbouring interesting displays of new paganism; would-be fauns and centauresses assembled in an air which was charged with "the frenzy of mute Saturnalia"; Wedekind made his Marquis von Keith say, "My whole talent rests upon the disagreeable fact that I cannot breathe a bourgeois atmosphere."

This is only the tiniest fragment of the anti-patriotic, anti-imperialistic, anti-bourgeois, cosmic, mystic, absolutistic art and literature which appeared in Germany under William II; a lyric phantom was walking through the full daylight of Wilhelminian success, melodiously or trenchantly whispering "pretence" into the ear of the bourgeois. But this was nothing in comparison with the pandemonium that started after the defeat of 1918. It has been said that half of the population of America is busy trying to sell something to the other half. In Germany after 1918 half of the population was busy telling the other half that it was bourgeois and not genuine. Art became a chamber of horrors, a purgatory, which the docile German was supposed to enter in order to rid his system of the bourgeois. There was no aspiring youth who would not attempt to make a different creature of himself than he really was in order to make the limited contemporaries gape. There were people who ate sand and apple peelings, and others who donned sandals and hairy shirts, and others who did not don anything at all. Roaming youngsters jumped through the fire, and starry-eyed oldsters planted cabbage in patterns suggested by astrology. There were individuals who liberated the essential in themselves through climbing impossible precipices, or fraternizing with lions in their cage, or becoming bullfighters, and others who looked like cubes and made hissing sounds.

Emerson describes a convention of Utopians he witnessed on sober American soil: "Madmen, madwomen, men with beards, Dunkers, Muggletonians, come-outers, Groaners, Agrarians, Seventh Day Baptists, Quakers; Abolitionists, Calvinists, Unitarians and Philosophers—all came successively to the top, and seized their moment, if not their hour, wherein to chide, or pray, or preach, or protest." If this can happen in America, expressionistic Germany of the twenties outdid the fakirs of India. Even the average German was persuaded that, to save his face, he had at least to behave as if he were an inhabitant of the All, instead of Germany. "Earth is a tellurian heaven"—a plethora of high-sounding slogans impressed visiting Americans like shrieks of exotic birds. Ehrenstein cried, "Pulverize the cities, smash the machine, dissolve the state." Becher sputtered a "Paean against the Age," and George Grosz industriously collected on the asphalt of Berlin upsetting details for the portrait of the bourgeois who refused to die.

Yes, the bourgeois refused to die. Gay little theatres, where once nothing more exciting happened than ceremonial escapes to the Isle de Cythères, staged extremist sons who murdered their bourgeois fathers; a most blatant, a most nauseating sensualism was advertised with the express purpose of smoking the impeccable bourgeois out, with the result that the bourgeois prospered because all this gave Berlin the reputation of being "the gayest city in Europe," and attracted clients from everywhere. Against the pious "hurrah patriotism" of the bourgeois the Treaty of Versailles was rationalized into a monument of triumphant bourgeois mentality. At the same time it was proclaimed with chiliastic fervor in the teeth of bourgeois callousness that "Man is good." Fraternizations among the genus man were recommended and practised in the face of bourgeois exclusiveness. Anti-capitalism was preached from every possible angle, the intellectual angle by philosophers like Scheler, the anthroposophical angle by Rudolf Steiner and his group, the political angle by the "Tat" circle of Fried, Zehrer, and others, the Christian angle by roaming Catholic and Protestant and free-lancing youth movements, the "Gestalt" angle by economists around Othmar Spann, the communistic angle, the fascist angle, the futuristic angle. In opposition to the stifling concept of the "maturity" of the bourgeois, the child was assiduously cultivated by educational reformers or by dadaists. In defiance of the "unrelieved and apathetic boredom" of the bourgeois' waking state, as Julian Green described it, the dream was rescued, put on a pedestal, and observed with applause and fascination. In place of the bourgeois' chilly utilitarian notions about history, a school of mythologists revealed the legendary character of creation. Against the bourgeois mania for a well-dusted Conditioned, Heidegger, Jaspers, and others raised the electric monotony of the Unconditioned, an existential philosophy. Men like Frobenius discovered the amazing symbolism of so-called backward tribes; the mighty accents of exotic continents were enthusiastically confronted in music and esthetics with the thin articles the bourgeois pretended to care for; dance, sport, and paradise were reinterpreted; poverty, which the bourgeois had treated as if it were leprosy, was made into a religion.

Alas, the effect of all this was the survival of the bourgeois, who was found in 1932, only slightly ruffled, hatching the egg of scarcity. All the clamor could not shake the bastille of bourgeois complacency, although a few lines by Beaumarchais had been enough, in the eighteenth century, to rock the edifice of the Ancien Régime.

However, in a most unexpected way this collective prayer for the liberation of the world from the tyranny of the price mechanism and its complacent priesthood—that is, in a way, from themselves—was fulfilled when the bottom was knocked out of the market in 1929. Insecurity was not liked any better than philistine security, unemployment was not more attractive than employment for unsatisfactory ends. With a determination born of despair, the ruins of complacency were rationalized into a façade of that higher spiritual independence which was so fervently sought for; but resentment very soon disfigured this artificial serenity.

In 1932 Germany looked a little like the abandoned cities of Asia, like Ayudhia, Angkor, and Pegu. Bats lived in factories, grass grew out of smokestacks, while thousands of homeless beings settled in woods and around lakes in much the same condition in which their ancestors had been, when they had arrived, clad in furs, from nowhere. These ancestors on the threshold of civilization had a greater chance for survival than their progeny on the threshold of twentieth century metropoles. The machine civilization is of grandiose and virile ugliness at its best; in its decay the ugliness becomes a perversion advertising itself. The ruins of static god-ridden civilizations make man creative, because they suggest the waste of a beautiful thought; ruins of machines suggest the vacuum which they have been unable to stop.

People with dishevelled hair, in outmoded attire, plucking a guitar saved from their *Wandervogel* days, like slaves of a modern Pharaoh whose ugly name was "No-Jobs" and who refused to build pyramids, were wandering endless miles toward some arid promise, some tiny spring, nay, drop, of activity; only to send word to their families that the inverted deluge, the total desert of unemployment, had not yet passed. These people noticed that law and reason were not "life-giving." What ends, they wondered, have they served? This question is the real revolution of our time, the Valmy of our century. The answer the Germans gave to this question through Hitler was disastrous. But what was the answer which the bourgeois gave?

There is a story of the wild-eyed poor man who came to

Rothschild and launched himself into an eloquent exposition of a Utopian creed, starting with "property is theft." At the end he asked for a share of Rothschild's fortune, whereupon the great banker reached into his pocket and gave him a cent. "If everybody on this earth would come into my office and ask for his share of my fortune, this is exactly what he could reasonably expect." But in 1932 a wild-eyed poor man would not have asked money from the rich man, he would have asked for work. He would not have minded at all the rich man's being rich, if that wealth had only been able to fill the air again with the throb of a functioning society. The poor man would have told the Rothschild of 1932 not, "You are a thief because you have property, therefore I want my share of your fortune"; but, "Be your worst, economic man, so that you can be your social best; use the freedom you have wrested from theocratic and feudal society and pursue your economic advantage with maddening persistency; show your teeth, great plutocratic ogre, and satiate your acquisitive instincts in the approved manner of your century as Tamerlane did it in the approved manner of his; be an economic Tamerlane, if this only means work for me."

But the Tamerlane of the twentieth century had no other wisdom to offer but to wait until the catastrophe of abundance had passed. Just as in a time of rising prosperity it had been to the advantage of the worker to withhold his commodity, work, at a time of declining prosperity it was to the advantage of the entrepreneur to withhold the goods which proved a veritable embarrassment of riches because they buried the price fetish under their profusion.

To cite once more the coffee thrown into the ocean, the grain burned while people clamored for bread is very much like whipping a dead horse; but it is a story which will become immortal because it sums up a certain absurdity in economic man's behaviour just as the necklace affair and the Bastille summed up certain undesirable traits of the Bourbon monarchy. Anyone who goes from house to house looking for a job, or who writes letters in every direction offering his services, and who with every negative answer or no answer at all becomes more convinced that the only social service expected of him is to commit suicide and thus cease to be a bother, must feel like the grain which Earth had miraculously conceived and developed so that it might become good white or black bread, but which, with all its fine energies, was committed to the flames because it happened to be a burden on the price. This is the kind of harvest festival that greeted the globe when it swelled the domain of man with gifts from the depths of existence. If nothing else, the panic into which the fit of tellurian fertility plunged mankind revealed the bankruptcy of imagination. The bourgeois had tamed Nature, and had burrowed diligently the channels into which the great creative mother was supposed to throw her fruits; but fertility proved unmanageable and got out of control. Thus the gigantic scheme failed because it worked too well; it worked so well that a growing number of unemployable men were facing a growing number of unsalable things.

It was a tug of war between a growing surplus of population and a growing surplus of things and foodstuffs. Ironically it appeared to be a Malthusian crisis in reverse: the growth of things not only equalled but outdistanced the growth of population. But this was no comfort so far as the price mechanism was concerned. In order to nurse prices, the indivisibility of existence, the philosophical fraternity that exists between the members of creation, was denied. Material growth, like inspiration, is something which rolls from an unknown centre into the planet Earth; man is not the creator but the receiver of it. Man builds the receptacle, the storehouse, the distributing centre of something that isn't man's. He is the broker of sidereal force, the dealer in an active force or entelechy which, though it is immensely older than the sun, unlike the sun is not losing its energy, and, no matter whether organic or inorganic creation, is not man's creation.

The globe did what she was asked to do, she surrendered her riches. Splendidly arrayed like a bride, she gave herself to her husband, as the Adriatic Sea glittered voluptuously when the Doge of Venice proclaimed himself the husband of those lovely and treacherous waves. But, alas, the globe chose as husband not a crowned actor intoxicated with his role, but a bourgeois. And the bourgeois did not embrace his glowing bride, literally fallen from heaven into his lap, without reserve and hesitation and with a grateful heart. He committed the biblical sin of Eulabeia or faintheartedness in a situation that called for the whole man. He applied to the charms of his immensely powerful and magnetic bride the well-known economic principle of time utility—he decided to store the charms away until a time when he could make use of them to better advantage. While he waited for this propitious time, he expected a sorely harassed state to pay him a pension.

Blaise Cendrars [6] and Stefan Zweig [7] tell us about the Swiss Sutter who owned the best land in California. Everything was fine until one day gold was found on his property. Theoretically Sutter was the richest man under the sun. But the news spread like wildfire, and Sutter's estate was overrun by a frantic mob of golddiggers. There was no longer any question of orderly management—cows perished unmilked, hogs died unfed, horses broke loose, crops were trampled under, pastures were inundated. Thousands of claims were feverishly established; only Sutter's supreme claim, Sutter's monopoly had a great fall, and though he moved heaven and hell, he could not bring it to life again. The life of the letter he held was too small compared with the life of the people who invaded the monopoly of the individual from Switzerland with the same anarchic directness with which the surpluses of population and commodities invaded the inherited conceptions of normalcy in 1932.

In 1932, meaninglessness seemed to celebrate an unholy marriage with joblessness. Had perchance the unemployment of the soul something to do with the unemployment of the body? From his steel-plated sanctum in Detroit Henry Ford had proclaimed: "Machinery is accomplishing in the world what man has failed to do by preaching, propaganda, or the written word—ushering in the United States of the World." Had the world-unifying machinery come to a stop because there was no unified thought behind it? Because preaching, propaganda, and the written word had failed to give machinery a universal and basic meaning? Because machinery unified only in appearance, but in fact the million disconnected, chaotic, petty, and thoughtless impulses which had scattered it over the earth cancelled out its unifying energies?

In 1932 precisely this was the question: Would it be possible to find a meaning for society vast enough, direct enough, yes, having enough of an anarchical directness to be able to overrule an old law, an old intricate and impotent sophistication, and to keep pace with the growing bounty of physical creation, with man and his harvests and riches? This meaning —in order to be effective, in order to halt the cutting up of the basic indivisibility of creation, in order to stop the faintheartedness in the face of great decisions, excuses for doing nothing, caution which shrank back from perspective—this meaning was bound to employ the unifying property of depth. Such a meaning, we need not emphasize, was not found in Germany in 1932. Naturally the bourgeois, constitutionally antagonistic to a deeper world view, did not foster it because he rightly assumed that it would be used against him, not in so far as he was man, but in so far as he was the self-appointed distributor of the bounty of creation. But the bourgeois was not saved by his faintheartedness. Hitler's bastard meaning was to expose in its own illiterate directness the vanity of individual monopolies and would-be monopolies—not against a background of depth, but against the background of another

# REVIVAL OF THE SPIRIT FAILS 129

surface, another monopoly, another exclusiveness, another division. The swing of the pendulum towards significance was broken.

No reservoir of depth prevented a horribly negative solution of the dilemma. During the last hundred years of progress, the dimension of depth had been so consistently derided and suppressed as the most impractical and obnoxious of all illusions that no jumping through fire or standing on the head could restore the power to draw lightning from the sky. In the end people doubted that it could be done. They too had read Spengler, and they began to believe him. No changes in the diet brought "Weimar" back, while the Nazis already erected their gibbets in panic-stricken suburbs.

There were still wood dwellers in 1932 who, like St. Augustine and Daumier, considered politics as such and business as such sheer idiocy—a latrocinium, a thieves' den, sound and fury, something not worth the bones of a Hottentot. The idea that one party should be better than another party, or good at all, seemed as ludicrous to them as the assertion that the left shoe is better than the right shoe, and of special significance. Their ambition was to resemble Dostoevsky, who took an interest in the soul but not in society, which had forgotten the soul. These unemployed, who had turned their plight into a virtue, felt as remote from the Treaty of Versailles as the man in the moon feels from the excitement on the stock market.

The idea of changing the Treaty of Versailles, so hotly advocated by Hitler, was to them escapism of the worst sort—a change rather of the environment than of the self. The world of unredeemed chance, the world that changes its frontiers every twenty-five years as a sick man changes his position in bed, was their enemy in every shape. It polluted the air with that meaninglessness for which Pascal found his famous simile: If Cleopatra's nose had been an inch longer, world history would have been different. It was meaninglessness that sent Cézanne before the Mont St. Victoire in Provence, the Sinai of modern art, where he prayed for the tables of Significance.

These people in the woods had wanted, in the heydays of expressionism, to think and feel "on the lines of the Architect of the Universe"; like embryos wrapped in the cosmic process, they wanted "to be lived" by the Whole. They had appreciated the activities of their fellow men only in so far as they were transported by them, as through the power of an oracle, into the right kind of imagination, into the right quality of happiness. Alas, the oracles, as Ivanov wrote to his friend in the other corner of the room, were "exhausted"; Plutarch, a Greek Spengler, has written a book on the subject.

Decidedly, meaning seems to have no chance between the devil of complacent reason and the deep sea of Hitlerian resentment. For anybody who believed in the musical genius of Germany—musical in the widest sense—the spectacle of Germany's spiritual fall was the greatest disappointment he could have experienced.[8]

# CHAPTER IV

## UTOPIAS WITHOUT SPIRIT

*Intellectual disgrace
Stares from every human face,
And the seas of pity lie
Locked and frozen in each eye.*

*Follow poet, follow right
To the bottom of the night,
With your unconstraining voice
Still persuade us to rejoice;*

*With the farming of a verse
Make a vineyard of the curse;
Sing of human unsuccess
In a rapture of distress;*

*In the deserts of the heart
Let the healing fountain start;
In the prison of his days
Teach the free man how to praise.*
—W. H. AUDEN,
*In Memory of W. B. Yeats* [1]

*Saints juifs, saints grecs, saints latins et romains, saints français; saints anglais et saints bourguignons—il n'y en a qu'une race qui est la race éternelle. Il n'y en a qu'une race qui est la race qui ne finira point; la race spirituelle; la race éternelle; qui ne finira jamais, éternellement jamais. Car elle procède, car elle vient de la source qui ne tarira éternellement jamais.*
—CHARLES PÉGUY, *Jeanne d'Arc* [2]

AGAIN I FEEL LIKE APOLOGIZING FOR HAVING BEEN SO impolite and possibly imprudent as to place in the centre of the formidable world crisis not our foes but you and myself, the bourgeois. There is, however, such a thing as beginning the re-education of our enemies with a re-education of ourselves. If world wars teach only the enemy a lesson, and nothing to us, then he is the winner, and we are the losers.

For a change I shall say something in favor of the status quo. The meaninglessness of the machine age is the peak of wisdom if the alternative is a fake meaning (for instance the racial myth) imposed on the long-suffering world with the help of machine guns. Liberalism recommended itself to the bulk of Western population as an escape from the atmospheric pressure of inwardness and medievalism. The Occident in general preferred the metropolitan chance world and irresponsibility to the stern exigencies of, say, Kantianism or New England Puritanism. And, it must be said, if liberalism is meaningless, it is almost divine in comparison with the meaning of terror. Anybody who lived under the totalitarian terror could hardly entertain higher hopes than to see the world purged from it. He would fasten the text of the Atlantic Charter on the bare wall of his study and he could not be blamed if he saw the solution in the negative act of eliminating the nightmare, in the "freedom from...."

The racial myth which we just mentioned served a very important purpose. In the storehouse of neutral power called the modern world, society is a more or less well-functioning machine. A machine has no other meaning but to function. If it does not function well, there is a possibility that the motor may be defective. The issue we shall discuss in the present chapter is the attempt to substitute, for the motor on which the non-totalitarian social machines were running none too smoothly about 1932, another motor so forceful that it gave the German social machine an extraordinary start. The non-totalitarian motor is the normal pressure of human appetites; but since the normal pressure was not enough to eliminate unemployment, the motor of the German social machine was charged with the abnormal pressure generated by militancy. The Nazi-pundits tried to fertilize the barren soil of the machine age with the adage, taken from Clausewitz but reversed, that politics is the continuation of war by different means.[3] The integration and animation which comes through the will to conquer a foe, presupposes a foe. The racial myth furnished the priceless substitute for meaning—an enemy. I submit that Hitler's enemy was the bourgeois masquerading as Jew, or the Jew masquerading as bourgeois. This anti-bourgeois revolt appealed even to the bourgeois because it was mature enough to have machine guns. Otherwise it would have been just another of the impotent trumpet blasts which failed to pulverize the walls of the middle-class Jericho.

The Nazis distributed sublime and infernal qualities among the races as the Calvinistic God distributes Grace. The "psycho-biological determinism," manipulated by Spengler to fit his morphological epic, was here used on the level of beer-hall brawls to absolve the Germans from the original sin of inferior motives and to burden the Jews with the world disaster of materialism. Because the Jew was by nature materialistic, and the German by natural predestination idealistic, the great quest of the doubting modern generation after significance was settled in a most gratifying way. Over night, certainty was recaptured. The obsessions of a frustrated putschist, an inflamed lowbrow, codified in the pages of *Mein Kampf*, became the law of the land. There was no more need for youngsters to jump through fires, to eat apple peelings, and to cultivate cubism and cabbage. Here at last was truth, and it was singularly fitted for the exigencies of the state machine.

Hobbes in his *Leviathan* [4] had already stipulated the interesting principle that a miracle is what the state decrees to be a miracle, in the same sense in which Goering reserved the right to decree who is an Aryan and who not. If it should suit a state that a circle is a square, then a circle is a square. "Authority, not Truth" is the Erastian dogma which endeavoured to bring the endless squabbles of theologians in the sixteenth century as safely to an end as the Nazi dogma actually ended the metaphysical operations on the German Blocksberg between 1920 and 1930. Because the aim of life is the manufacture of results, lies, being most effective in this connection, are manufactured into eternal verities.

The worst that can be said against the Jews is that they enacted, like the Germans, the fallen angel. The parallel between the two self-styled chosen peoples, the Germans and the Jews, is striking. Originally they were both prisoners of their taboos. If the irrational ground that gives meaning to their collective lives is impaired, the catastrophe is comparable to the death of the queen in a beehive. "The populations of Oceania," we read in the Geography of Reclus, "are fast dying out for they have lost the body of ideas which governed their actions." [5] The demon in Jewish and German brains—which arranged the phenomena of the world in violently perfumed bouquets of *Weltanschauungen* which looked like a Wagnerian opera or like Jehovah's despotism—was killed by the modern age. Machine, money, reason killed the selective principle, the tribal temperament that saw the world as a distinct pattern. The patterns of course differed as widely as Nordic woods differ from Palestinian deserts. But the atmospheric pressure that forced the world like a hallucination upon the brains of Germans and Jews was similar. Even the pattern often coincided. Germans and Jews are anti-classical peoples, ridden by the "fear of the Lord," groping, in fits of spiritual persecution mania, for shelter where the glowing arrows of the Creator's wrath cannot reach them; and yet, once the angel with whom they used to wrestle evaporates in the chilly light of reason, they are seized by nostalgia for the tyrannical weight of mystery; the void into which they are liberated gives them agoraphobia, and they flee into space, into methods of controlling the tangible world, with a "superlative of energy that transcends the purpose." [6]

The mighty voice that talked out of clouds and from the peaks to the Hebrews found an overwhelming echo in the Germans. In the holy time of incubation, about A.D. 1000, when the medieval scene was roughly staked off by augur-eyed emperors and monks roving through goblin-infested thickets between the Rhine and Vistula, the apocalyptic visions of Daniel, Isaiah, Ezekiel, and St. John the Divine reverberated in Germany more than in any other European country. Even France at that time could not match the fervor with which the German, by a kind of elective affinity, turned toward the burning bush of Jewish transcendentalism. On the island of Reichenau in the Lake of Constance, where the landscape reminds one of a Theocritan idyl transported to the northern slopes of the Alps, the monks about A.D. 1000 illuminated books with paintings which had nothing of the lofty harmony of the Logos, but everything of sheer Judaic awe and obsession. The miniatures of Reichenau show the sublime terror of a soul that is swallowed by the Universe as Jonah is by the whale and that like Jonah feels the approaching dawn of resurrection.

On the Bernward door at Hildesheim, which is of the same time, one sees Adam and Eve, not elegant Greek nudes but human straws in the wind, trembling in an eerie infinity through which the Demiurge swims like a leviathan. Thus German expressionism found its climax nine hundred years before it became an industry. It was not classic poise that Luther preached, but Jehovah at his most arbitrary, the abyss ever ready to eat the children of his Saturnian whim. In *De Servo Arbitrio*, Luther's answer to the civilized Erasmus, the reformer almost revels in describing the horrifying, most un-Christian attribute of Jehovah, the Jewish tribal god who became, instead of Wotan, the tribal god of the Germans, trampling on his children as if they were grapes, a God who also appealed in his Old-Testamentarian grandeur to the English and Scotch non-conformists more than he did in his avatar as the all-loving Father of Christianity.

Both the German and the Jewish systems are envenomed or enlivened—whichever way you prefer—by the urge to protest. James Darmestetter [7] wrote in the nineties that "Jehovah was a centre of protest against the more refined and materially superior civilization of the Phoenicians." Thomas Mann, in the "unpolitical" book he composed during the first world war, maintained that Luther's protest against the indifference of civilization, a protest so dear also to the slavophiles, was the typical attitude of the German. It has been said about the courtiers who were meandering around Francis I that they "concentrated on the trivial in order to emphasize the unimportance of the serious."[8] Nothing could better express the condition which made the Jews of antiquity anti-Hellenistic and anti-Roman, and the Germans of modernity anti-Western, and the rest of the world, as a reaction, anti-Semitic and anti-German. It is the protest of peoples who live in dangerous currents, who cry out as if lost in the labyrinth of their hallucinations, and are grieved to observe that their neighbours are far from sharing their apprehensions. They protest against what they think is too easy a solution of the difficult human equation. It has often been asked why Jews were so prominent in the expressionistic Germany between 1920 and 1930, or rather since 1900. Germans and Jews both met in protest against the emptying of the world—they protested that the world was emptying itself not in the sense of Master Eckhart so that God might dwell in it unobstructed by human follies, but in the sense that the world might not be bothered by God any longer.

The deep-rooted spiritual affinity between Germans and Jews was clearly demonstrated—as if it needed to be demonstrated—in the protesting Germany of the twenties. The German-Jewish combination worked while there was hope that the gap between mechanism and organism, so typical for the modern world, could be overcome in the unifying dimension of depth. In 1932 this hope had vanished, and the only way to bring meaning back to the disintegrated human herd seemed a blind assertion of the will in the dimension of the surface, the particular tribe. A radical separation of the partners recommended itself to the "new cannibalism" which put all other "isms" to flight. The three great neuters, machines, intellect, and money—against whose general predominance Jewish authors like Werfel, Doeblin, Kornfeld, Buber, had protested just as eagerly as their Aryan colleagues—were made into specific media of corruption operated by the Sages of Zion for the benefit of the Jews against the character of rival tribes.

The Jewish tribe was accused of making dissolvents of tribal innocence their specialty. Can anything be simpler? The involved panorama of modernism, the roaring metropoles and the mad jerks of the motorized centipede of civilization are nothing but the empty grimace of a disillusioned ethnical group. This theory localizes the bourgeois, an international phenomenon, and his complement, the Marxist, in a nation without locale, namely the Jews. The despair and the vices of a world which had lost its meaning thus became part of the grand strategy of a fiendish tribal ambition. The German of course argued himself free from any responsibility in a situation which he hated because it exploded his own chosen-people complex. He may have outwardly embraced materialistic and mechanistic habits himself, he may have diluted his tribal purity by rootless hedonism; if so, he was merely the victim of a dangerous rival whose hedonism and materialism were not thoughtlessness but method—a rival tribe which saw in the internationalism of the twentieth century the expression of its own very special nationalism.

Here we are interested only in the attempt on the part of the Nazis to exploit the atavistic anti-Jewish panic to the detriment of bourgeois civilization. The feeling of the Germans that "they are not understood," that they are "different," that they are strangers in the modern world, that the machine age is not "natural," not "organic" was suddenly explained: Germany and all "decent" peoples were the victims of a conspiracy from familiar quarters. The severance of the spiritual partnership between Germans and Jews was essentially a simplification of the complex anti-bourgeois tradition for the sake of action, a monstrous *sacrificium intellectus;* it was a reinstatement of the practical, which expressionism had treated like a Cinderella, into its proper element, resentment and complacency.

We have said that the Jew acted the fallen angel. This is true. Once the German and the Jew leave the heaven of spiritual tension and try their hand in earthly matters, they throw themselves into the arena with an uncanny energy "which transcends the purpose." Like deep-sea fish that cannot live near the surface, they longed madly for the lost pressure. The Germans and Jews build up pressures artificially in the effort to drown the rebellious voices of their neglected metaphysical duties. There is something grim in the way they enter competition, and display their satisfaction after a victory is won. For the Germans this is true even without wars, which are merely the most drastic means of forgetting spiritual homelessness in a hypertrophy of action. In his pamphlet, *The Causes for Germanophobia*, published during the first world war, the philosopher Max Scheler ascribed the phenomenon of anti-Germanism to the aggressive interpretation of work prevalent in the fatherland.

The spiritual homelessness of the Jews is indicated by the nervous exaggeration with which this solemn old race of patriarchs forces itself to take success seriously in an antispiritual society. Having been frozen into an introverted exclusiveness for millenniums, they persuade themselves, once the hypnosis which has kept them mummified is gone, that to concentrate, like Francis I and his courtiers, "on the trivial in order to emphasize the unimportance of the serious," is liberty. There is no need to point out that this attitude is passionately combated by Jews like Buber, Waldo Frank, and a thousand others. As an aside, it deserves mention that in 1938, in Nazi Germany, a German nature philosopher, Edgar

Dacqué, published a book, *The Lost Paradise*, which, partially based on the research of Goldberg (*Wirklichkeit der Hebräer*), presented the viciously externalized Germans with a portrait of the "Magic Israel" which used to make itself into a "body of the Lord." The publication of this book at that particular moment rather ironically recalled the *Germania* by which Tacitus tried to improve his likewise viciously externalized countrymen through a portrait of the tribal innocence of the Germans. There is hardly a doubt, however, that a great percentage of Jews, taking advantage of the liberalism of the last hundred and fifty years, have enjoyed acting the "fallen angel." And, seeing thus in a mirror his own spiritual decay, his own impotence to call upon the forces of the deep, the kind of German who avoids humble self-scrutiny at all events —of whom the Nazi is the epitome—would hate the Jew as a pleasant alternative for hating himself.

The fact remains that certain frustrated German ex-expressionists and ex-everything felt impelled to challenge, when they scratched the skin of plutocracy and Marxism and discovered the Jew, the age in which they were living in the Jewish image. The French Revolution that had introduced this age into Europe became Jewish, the religion which this age professed became Jewish, the law which held this age together became Jewish. Physics, mathematics, the law of gravitation became Jewish.

The quality of German protests deteriorates decidedly as time advances. During the first world war, one of Germany's finest young scholars, Norbert von Hellingrath, expressed his pained surprise at the naïveté with which German professors announced in 1914 that Goethe was marching with Big Bertha against the West. Goethe at least has been spared the doubtful privilege of serving as ammunition in the second world war. If this looks like commendable advance towards candor, it reveals in reality only the fact that the spokesmen of the Nazis were officially preferred to Goethe. It is surely a sad comment on the logic of history that nine hundred years of exercises in detachment, of moving the soul through all the narrow passes and on all the high mountains that it might have its uttermost freedom and feel its ultimate power, that this pilgrimage—not nobler than the pilgrimage of any other people, and yet not less noble—should result in a poisonous fog in whose night an ancient continent expires. These are no small matters. People will have to search for the causes of this phenomenon, and find them, and adjust themselves accordingly. It is no small matter that a tribalism of a particularly bestial kind should have appeared preferable to the lessons of nine hundred years of training in the unifying qualities of depth. Man must have uttered a horrible Sesame that the stones and colors and sounds and letters and the very rivers and rocks and forests which used to evoke generous echoes in human hearts—and to re-echo the fairy tales and confessions, miracles and songs which they had evoked—could not keep Hell from opening its gates and the demons from trampling this great wealth under their feet.

In 1933 the Germans, in trying to regain the atmospheric pressure without which they could not act, resorted to war against the Jews. They made war against what we have called the "fallen angel" type, the citizen and promoter of the unified secularized modern world, who feeds the centipede of civilization with an excess of energy typical for newcomers, a very German as well as a Jewish phenomenon. But in order to do this, and to find strength in the protest against the unification of the world through machine and money, the German had also to make war against the unification of the world through German and Jewish metaphysics. This meant they had to make war against the most precious contributions of both Germans and Jews, because it was here that rose the glorious sun of universalism, whose warm rays pierced the hard shell of tribal isolation.

Leon Roth, in an essay in *The Legacy of Israel*,[9] has made a great case for the spirit of "Wholeness" in the Jewish tradition, the "Unity of control" guaranteed by monotheism, the *natura naturans* penetrating the smallest particle of the great cosmic cake as leaven. "To interpret the universe in the light of human opinions is to Hebraism ultimate blasphemy." Jewish pundits like Maimonides, Spinoza, Bergson, Alexander, and Freud are quoted as rebels, in the interest of an absolute view, against anthropomorphic final causes—an idea borne out by Goethe's remark in *Dichtung und Wahrheit* on Spinoza. Einstein's theory is characterized as an "attempt to get behind the limited point of view of the individual observer—a further step towards the depersonalization of our fundamental ideas." The meaning of this is that Jewish tribalism is complemented and rounded out by a tendency to integrate the limited human situation in an enormous panorama both complex and homogeneous. The revolution of the Cosmic Christ against an exclusive and sectarian definition of the Absolute in the Jewish community would thus express the essential trait in the Jewish character. In this sense Maritain may be right when he says, speaking on the subject of anti-Semitism, that the movement is really inspired by a hatred of Christ. It is the genius that encompasses the sum total of Being without exception in one sweeping inspiration—"L'amore que move il sole e l'altre stelle"—which makes the traffickers in particulars shudder.

The Nazis then attacked the feverish loyalty of modern Jews to mammonized machine civilization, a loyalty which has irked many worthy people immensely but which, as we have seen, was no less typical of the German middle class. And they linked this loyalty for a profitable and homeless neuter to that other tendency of Judaism—the universalistic tendency of which Christianity is the climax. For the sake of militancy and atmospheric tension it was boundaries that were wanted. Therefore the superficial unification through the machine and the profound unification through the spirit were coupled together and both condemned.

Against the siren song of the Absolute, intoned in Germany by both Germans and Jews during the fantastic 1920's, the Nazis vindicated the claims of the conditioned. The unconditioned in any form—the Jews offered two aspects of it, money and spirit—was the enemy, because it eliminated the focus where man's tellurian energies could gather and strike out in blind, primeval lust. Civilization—a carefully distilled set of circumstances, matter in motion, property, cause and effect, security, police, "scientific humanism," "human engineering"—was a neutral force transcending organic boundaries. It had been attacked, without result, in the twenties, from the standpoint of the "music which extinguishes civilization." Now it was attacked from the standpoint of the particular, and lo, the amorphous and broken-down organization of the modern world revived around defiant centres.

In the competition to find a meaning around which the great ailing neuter of civilization could crystallize anew, to find a cause for which the machine of civilization could work again, the denial of the unconditioned carried the day over the party which wrote the unconditioned on its banner—the party which insisted that any other solution would not be "true" in the twentieth century. All the Nazis had done was this: They had changed the moribund particular of the economic man, his sovereign self-interest which, once stopped by depression, was unable to make the wheels turn, into the hectic particular of the tribe, and now things started rolling again. Work was salvaged not by a re-appreciation of the "great fact of existence" as such: but the hellish power of resentment wanted a body, and the Nazis were only too glad to lend their physique.

A Utopia was coming to life in Central Europe. J. M. Keynes had written about the time when the great crisis about 1930 reached the peak of its dismal career: "The only way out is for us to discover some object which is admitted even by the deadheads to be a legitimate excuse for largely increasing the expenditure of someone on something." After Hitler took over, someone increased expenditure on something. This was an impressive fact. Visitors from abroad flocked to Berlin and many chose to broadcast to the world that things were happening. *Révolution de travail*, the Frenchmen called it, the revolution of work, and it was impossible to designate in more tempting form the revolution that was needed in 1933.

Sophisticated globe trotters from Paris, whose own Promethean urge for work had been partly exhausted by the lucrative activities of their fathers, made the tour of the salons of Berlin, calling Hitler "Jean d'Arc." The abyss of unemployment was filled in; the caste system disappeared; and, if you could only forget the ranting of the Austrian medicine man for a moment or the enormous injustices committed in his name, you might have had a vision of a Carlylean concept of work reigning supreme in the heart of Europe.

Even in the House of Lords gentlemen who had passed a few weeks in a German spa under the swastika voiced their admiration, and denounced Hitler's critics as professional Cassandras or worse. Hitler challenged the mechanics of egoism and the hedonism of the "Jazz Age" by boldly informing his followers that they could not hope for better wages, but had to be content with the satisfaction derived from a heroic consciousness. He reaped frenetic applause. The German Utopia seemed to differ from the Utopian brotherhoods of old, like Brook Farm, Menilmontant, and Fourier's Phalanges, only in that it was successful.

Yet, paradoxically, it was successful because it was false, because it relied once more on the particular, only in a viciously aggravated form, against the spirit of the twentieth century which approaches the unconditioned from all sides. In the foreword to *Battle against Time* Heinrich Hauser, after giving a catalogue of astounding achievements, writes, "There is a deep tragedy in the fact that a great nation is making the most enormous efforts and undergoing the most severe deprivations for a cause which is in itself fundamentally false." [10] It was fundamentally false because it signified the sanctification of the surface where distinctions multiply—the surface and its distinctions no longer tempered by the waves from the receding deep which still had washed the shores of liberalism. Moby Dick, the great white whale, "that lonely phallic monster of the individual you," [11] had been, like the Babylon of Revelation, enthroned as supreme generator of vital energies.

A genuine Utopia cannot be but unconditioned; because it is an absolute it must correspond to the absolute; because it means peace in permanence it cannot be based upon the deification of the particular. The deification of Moby Dick ended, as we are all too aware, with the pulverization of Moby Dick. The particular as the ultimate source of conduct has joined the procession of the dead who have been sacrificed in the second world war because the particular was allowed to survive too vehemently in the machine age. Mankind, its body unified by the machine, will perish if it retains the pride of its many heads and minds, and if it acts out the whims and lusts of a hydra, the multiplicity of mutually hostile natures.

Can we be sure that this is more than mere statement? Before my mind is not only the catastrophe of the particular—the particular nation, the particular doctrine and order—but also the catastrophe suffered by a mode of life based on the universal, on inward "growth of meaning," the epic of frustration which I have tried to sketch in the foregoing chapter. How can we hope that the particular will die after the Nazi particular is eliminated? Is not Spengler's idea, that the inward spells have dissolved and have to be supplanted by activities in space, the dominant idea which our epoch has thoroughly accepted? Is not the sport of becoming a particular, dissociated from the whole, and acquiring military and economic power, and exercising this particular power by expanding in space—is not this the dominant sport? What shall we do, as individuals and as tribes, if this sport is taken away from us? We feel almost like Wyndham Lewis when he is asked to give up the British Empire for the sake of seeing the Absolute in a davenport. And what if this Absolute is only an illusion? Not everybody has had the opportunity to stand before the Cathedral of Chartres, and if he has, most likely he did not have the eyes to see.

However, there is a general consensus of opinion that the particular has to give up its sovereignty in the machine age, just as the members of an international federation eventually have to sacrifice their sovereignty—the main objection of isolationists everywhere. But is a peace meaningful that is forced upon us mainly for the negative reason that man in the machine age has become too vulnerable to make martial enterprises pay? Can we act on a universal plane with the dynamic particular that gave spice to our lives blotted out, unless we are saints? Furthermore, a society of saints may have meaning, but it will bring the machines to a stop, because saints are not in need of many goods and have no money anyway. The machines will run only if the individual appetite is encouraged to assert itself. What will happen then, both Taoists and St. Francis have said in identical terms: First you have property, then you have weapons to defend that property, and then you have war.

The problem is the machine. Before we had the machine, even murderous particulars could run their course, and time and imagination would catch up with them eventually and give them their blessing because the catastrophes remained on a human scale. Or whole tribes could become saintly if they wished because their asceticism would not knock the bottom out of the market. But now, because the interdependence and closeness of the machine age makes any thorough indulgence in the whims and grandeurs of the particular suicidal, there will be people who will advocate scrapping the machine altogether; since man cannot be man in the machine age, it will be said it is better to get rid of the machine than of man.

In that Midway of overheated imagination, the Germany of the twenties, such ideas were widely popular. Ernst Toller, for instance, wrote a bad play on the Luddites, *The Machine-Smashers*. The machineless island of Bali was the object of a veritable cult—and rightly so, from all I can judge, having lived there three weeks, for each day was like a choric offering thrown into the lap of the gods. But even in hardheaded America, Stuart Chase compared the plight of "Middletown" during the depression with the dignified peace in which the "machineless men" of lonely Tepoztlan in Mexico lived.[12] "As new forms of life emerge, new parasites appear for their bedevilment. The business cycle is the microbe especially created to plague, if not ultimately to kill, the vast sprawling body of mechanical civilization. In this body, Middletown is but a single cell, while Tepoztlan is aloof and unincorporated, an organic breathing entity." Through Stuart Chase, Tepoztlan, unaffected by the cursed interdependence of modern economic processes, became the Bali of America.

Nevertheless, scrapping the machine—a gesture by which the dragon of greed would presumably be as incompletely slain as the dragon of discord was slain by scrapping the privileges of the French nobles in 1789—cannot be expected. But why have meaning at all? Why should we not see in the decadence of the wayward soul, and in the ascendancy of mechanical objectivity, a delivery from chance, and a victory of logic? Why should we insist, against Spengler and appearances, that the soul lives on in our time, though doomed like a butterfly in a waste of concrete? Why not take the cue from the machine and rebuild society around some core that is precise, and whose meaning is the pure logic of its functioning, instead of making its nucleus some steaming Pythian oracle, or tribal intuition, or atavistic loyalty? Diego Rivera's frescoes in California and Detroit introduce the slightly reluctant citizen to the cult of the modern Mithras and Isis—the dynamo and the laboratory.

Even when Germans worship something as rational as the machine, they are irrational. Nietzsche occasionally turned out glittering sentences in honor of the machine because its root is the "lessening of man," which he needed so that the pendulum could gather momentum for its backward or forward swing into the neighbourhood of the superman. But in America, Russia, and England attempts to turn society into an engine were made in a rational vein.

Let me mention three instances of social engineering, three visions which seem exactly to correspond to the necrologue Spengler delivered twenty-five years ago over the dead body of Europe's metaphysical glory: the social philosophies of Veblen, Lenin, and J. M. Keynes. They look like applications of the Spenglerian philosophy, based on the frank acknowledgment that man's inner processes have died; they differ from Spengler only in that the social engines do not find their justification in being driven permanently against each other by organized hatred and calculated combativeness; they are static. If mechanical logic can insure permanent peace where logic of the heart has failed, is it not madness to scrap the machine and become man? Should we not rather scrap man and become machine—the "homme machine" of Lamettrie?

First let us consider technocracy. As I understand Veblen, this yogi economist, the smiling sphinx from Minnesota, he was profoundly upset by the persistence of the "individual you" in a setting which was objective and unconditioned—but unconditioned not in the mystic sense of the deep, against which Hitler was to raise the horrible bogey of the surface; unconditioned in that the world was merely an extension of the machine.

The bourgeois had become the exponent of the machine—

"materialistic, unmoral, unpatriotic, undevout." The bourgeois in action was responsible for the great refutation of emotional significance, he had been the great nihilist and iconoclast who marched society from its highly symbolic and idyllic setting to the awful uniformity of the obvious, the tangible, the matter of fact and nothing but matter.

Veblen calls it the "reduction of the universe to the morally and esthetically colorless terms of the mechanical engineer." He, like Spengler, exhorts us to accept the heartbreak house of modern prose. He seems to cry, "Accept the machine age for what it is worth; put the instrument you created to adequate uses; don't make it subservient to foolish and outmoded superstitions; don't try to justify it through sentimental waste and subjective antics." But the bourgeois is no ascetic technocrat. Every day, or better every afternoon at five o'clock, the engineer, who performs his task objectively in the focus of a superhuman economic rhythm, slips back into the shell of the exhausted bourgeois longing for all-too-human relaxation. And the course of empires is as much dictated by the anti-climax as by the climax.

Veblen hunted the innumerable Moby Dicks splashing most irrationally in the ocean of modern efficiency. Inside his business office the bourgeois is the agent of the blind will of the physical Universe to advance in terms of the planet Earth; he pours the battalions of power he has at his command into the grand strategy of a universal process, "ushering in the United States of the World" according to Ford; but outside the office he is unable to abdicate. He needs the "individual you" as an antidote against the impersonality of the process, and too tired to live up to the reality of his situation, he looks for opportunities to re-inflate his personality which the pressure of impersonal work has flattened like a pancake.

Veblen was concerned with the determinants of bourgeois consumption, the problem of what mysterious agents called the glittering windows of Fifth Avenue into being, made rubber trees weep latex in inaccessible jungles, brought consternation and death to ostriches and paradise birds, distilled a drop of perfume from ten thousand roses or, as the chef of the Prince de Soubise boasted, a sauce from ten thousand hams. To look into the matter was to become convinced that mankind was using the magnificent tool of modern scientific organization in the same frame of mind that made the Roman Caesars employ the priceless skill of their engineers to erect amphitheaters in which human beings were devoured by monsters imported by an admirable system of communications; or to organize markets so that Trimalchio might have his dinner. In the words of Soddy: The pearls of science have been thrown to the swine.

Veblen was shocked that, in spite of everything, so many unscientific pretenses in a time like ours persisted; his remedy is *tabula rasa*—the acceptance of the fact that there is no meaning beyond the law of cause and effect. He stops short of making a *Weltanschauung* of his discovery; to him it is merely a problem of efficient economics.

Can the unconditioned be realized on the surface? So far as it is matter, yes; but not so far as it is life—which on the surface is a colony of Moby Dicks, of individual wills. If you cannot reach objectivity through spirit you reach it through matter. A superlative of materialism—not anthropocentric indulgences, but a conscious identification with the cohesion and necessity of matter—cannot fail to become unconditioned. But life is left out in the open.

Veblen and his school propagated a streamlined industrial community, "conceived as one vast enterprise in which all members of industrial society are workers and share holders in common." There is no mistake as to what technocracy is out to suppress: the unscientific "rubbish of ideologies," the witches' sabbath of pampered private egoism, of little pretentious particulars. But Veblen's positive myth is pale: he relies on an instinct for workmanship and organization. It is well to remember that Veblen's Utopia has not been tried out in practice.

Veblen's technocratic Utopia and Lenin's communistic Utopia—not the actual U.S.S.R. but the world after the "withering away" of the state—differ from the reality of the complacent bourgeois as well as from the now tottering reality of the resentful fascist, both realities based on the particular, in so far as they attempt to eliminate the element of folly, of surprise, of uncontrolled historical eruptions. They are "scientific." The idea of cozy sentimentalism, "my home is my castle," and of gentlemanly independence is as repellent to both as is the theory of "dangerous living," and the irrational atavisms of the "blood and soil" dogma. The technocrats maintain that a second industrial revolution is needed, one whose object is a world definitely purged from all phantoms of the past, which so far have refused to die. This is the process in which we are engaged in the twentieth century, or should be engaged. It is social engineering relying on the assumption that man, trained by the precision and logic of the machine, will rather cease to be human than to be inefficient.

On the other hand, Marx's and Lenin's Utopias—a classless and stateless world—are scientific because they are the ineluctable consequence of the socio-economic philosophy on which Marxism rests, and in which Marxists believe.

Both Utopias, once realized, do without coercive measures. Veblen introduced the engineer, not the policeman; Lenin "demanded the immediate introduction of a system under which all should fulfill the functions of control and supervision, all should be bureaucrats for a time and therefore no one could become a bureaucrat." The scrubwoman would do as well as Pericles and Bismarck, as a matter of fact she would do better, because Pericles and Bismarck would be out of place but the scrubwoman would not. Thus Socratic optimism, which believes that anybody who "knows" what is best for him will "do" what is best for him, has found its standard bearers among the scientific minds of our sceptical time.

If we look for the integrating nucleus in these Utopias we find the principle of organization. It is possible to see, in the efficiency by which human wants are catered to on a global scale, a task both worthy and fascinating, a task in itself. It is possible to conceive of mankind as a co-operative devoted to perfecting this supreme task, which as time passes will evolve from very imperfect solutions to better solutions, just as a long succession of doses of intelligence and labor had to be applied to a motorcar model 1900 to make a motorcar model 1940. Yet it is obvious, if such a naïve statement can be tolerated, that these Utopias are not friendly to the theory of initiation which Ivanov defended against the *tabula rasa* doctrine of his friend Gershenson. The scientific Utopias admit, *sub rosa* but unmistakably, that the enemy is the man of the past, the irrational creature whose ossified conceits the bourgeois—out of malice, or mental laziness, or snobbery—has prolonged into the scientific era, where they are as much out of place as the Spanish court ceremonial is at a labor meeting. The condition *sine qua non* of these Utopias is that historical man as an obstacle to perfect machine-like efficiency and behaviour has to be eliminated.

The significance of these Utopias is that they are weapons in the hands of reformers, they are statements of a militant criticism; their realization, however, would be a major catastrophe. It would mean that the secularized fact of anthropocentric society would be worshipped on the altar of insufficient meaning. I remember living in a town in a Near Eastern country suddenly seized by a mania for progress, where the installation of a bathtub in the local hotel was made the occasion for a public celebration from which no patriot could well afford to absent himself. Much as the bathtub eventually contributed to the polish of my outward being, the inward being is loath to prostrate itself before the paraphernalia of plumbing. What greater satisfaction could be reserved to the society envisaged by the Utopias we have mentioned than the award of a gold or silver medal to a unit of production which turned out a million pins more than the Office for Pin Production had thought it capable of? Every move is controlled by a scientifically trained consciousness. "Functionalism," sighs a loyal citizen of Soviet Russia, "means one authority when a hand is to lift food to the mouth, another when it is to write a report and still another when it has to hit somebody in the face." [13] Even death cannot be invoked to deliver man from himself. "Fear of death," wrote Trotsky in the days of his glory, "will ultimately become nothing else but the useful reaction of the organism when encountering danger." [14]

Whitman, Hugo, and Shelley had magnificent visions of how great man would be in the twentieth century. It is tragic that the impossibility of avoiding a scientifically "lessened" man at every step makes the Utopias of Veblen and Lenin so unattractive. They may improve upon political realities which are based on the "individual you"—singular and collective; yet their scientific objectivity is nonetheless nothing but the glorification of a "lessened" creature. Very much like a German architect in the twenties, Trotsky—whose romanticism on the subject of human reason was eclipsed by no professional romanticist—saw mountains moved, not by faith but by more tangible techniques. "Man will take up the regrouping of mountains and rivers and will correct nature until he will have transformed her according to his image." Where are the guarantees that the world made over after the image of a communist will be an improvement? Every mountain will be a Mt. Rushmore bearing the likeness of the party leader, or at least his favorite slogan as a shallow *mene tekel*. It will be a triumph, but it will be essentially the same triumph that made us rebel against the complacency of the bourgeois who could not see the infinity of the ocean because of swimming Ritz-

Carlton restaurants. The Chinese, too, with their "Feng-shui," regrouped mountains and rivers, but it was a regrouping in the imagination, aided by a few wisely chosen and distributed accents, a thank offering to the spirit of harmony which outwits pride by intuition. Man withdrew by it into a transparent power where he was no longer necessary; feeling celestial aid, he was glad that he was not reminded of himself. He made himself beautifully invisible.

Veblen's and Lenin's Utopias are based on a belief that man can be perfected until his irrational components have worn off, and that it is worth while to impose his rationality with cast-iron rigidity upon the world. These Utopias differed from the laissez-faire world by asceticism, a militant grimness, a ruthless suppression of that faintheartedness so typical of the bourgeois in a crisis, and a strict egalitarianism—at least in theory. They stipulate that man in a mature world is no longer a political but a productive animal. Their integrating myth is therefore an instinct for workmanship and organization and efficiency, which is rationally exploited and becomes the guiding habit. Yet they suffer from an overdose of "lessened" man.

Perhaps we may now take a third Utopia under consideration, Mr. Keynes's ideas for a post-war world. Here we breathe freer, it is a gayer scene, it is as if we passed from a Cromwellian atmosphere into the presence of Nell Gwyn, with all the lights of the Restoration burning. Keynes also attacks the timidity of the bourgeois, but from a different angle—more in the manner of a young cavalier who, surrounded by tempting possibilities for carnal digressions and diversions, is pained by the budget consciousness and pedantic reticence of his parsimonious parents. The most sacred tenets of Puritan righteousness are thrown to the winds: hoarding is a vice, spending is a virtue.

A laissez-faire world which has reached its extensive margin, with no new continents to discover and to settle, and the moon out of reach, and the population by necessity and through various devices becoming stationary, cannot invest all its savings profitably. Money is hoarded and becomes dear, prices correspondingly fall, business activity slows down, the volume of production is reduced, and the *danse macabre* of unemployment starts anew. On the other hand, the greater the national income, the greater the volume of savings, and the more new investment is required. Everything depends therefore on investment; if people fail, for one or the other reason, to invest, the "circuit flow of money" is interrupted, the government has to step in, and, rather than let money stay idle, has to tax it away and invest it itself. Somewhere there is also a consumer who is burdened with the patriotic duty to absorb the results of this frantic investment policy, unless we are to call in earthquakes and wars whose competence in this context is unquestioned.

The Keynes Utopia, a government-directed spending spree, a spiral of prosperity strictly planned and kept under control, does not impolitely supplant the laissez-faire economy; but having, very much like Lenin and Veblen, a stationary world as its premise, it is fundamentally distinct from the liberal economy whose element is, or was, expansion. This is a point to be remembered. On the other hand, to discipline man into the "homme machine" of Veblen's and Lenin's Utopias is almost a moral achievement compared to the utter aimlessness of the Keynes world, where all the wild wasteful ways of the leisure class Veblen so unkindly exposed are welcome as potent stimulants for the failing demon Work. It is no longer a race between demand and production, but between unemployment and production. All the human follies Veblen and Lenin were so determined to expel are ceremoniously received as honored guests in the mansion of Mr. Keynes; the shallowest ostentation, if it only keeps mankind busy, will be accommodated in the *chambre de parade*. Alas, Mr. Keynes's faith in the capacity of his fellow citizens to develop Neronic complexes as a panacea against idleness is feeble; the state, possibly deprived of war-making, will have to embark upon projects of gigantic emptiness; everybody knows Keynes's recommendation to the treasury to "fill old bottles with banknotes, bury them at suitable depths in disused coal mines, which are then filled up to the surface with town rubbish, and leave it to private enterprise on well-tried principles of laissez-faire to dig the notes up again." Edward Hallett Carr, who quotes this passage in his impressive survey, *Conditions of Peace*,[15] adds sorrowfully that the fallacy underlying such schemes is not economic but moral.

Dostoevsky relates that it was one of his most melancholy experiences in Siberia when a mad overseer forced the convicts to transport a sandheap from one corner of the prison yard to the other and back again. The futility of the operation demoralized everybody. It is perhaps a compliment to our time that mankind is willing, if Mr. Keynes is right, to pay for the privilege of working with the acknowledgment of the hollowness of its doings. In earlier days, those who could not find work died or emigrated; in the Keynes Utopia they are kept alive and stay where they are (because there is no place to go) by means of a philosophy that substitutes for organic meaning the mechanism of a teeter-totter: one beam registers the pull of joblessness and the other the pull of jobs. The success of society will be measured by the equalization of the two pulls.

One generation having overhauled our cities, the next generation can think of nothing better than to overhaul them again, and so forth. Trotsky, as we have seen, supplies the additional idea of moving the mountains to where they look better. It is perhaps disappointing that William James's essay, *A Moral Equivalent of War*, brilliant as it is in opening the discussion when the issue was still young, does not proffer any solutions which lie beyond the province of the economist: slum clearing, etc.

The Utopias of Veblen, Lenin, and Keynes are conceived in opposition to the moral and idealistic "pretences" of the bourgeoisie, which prefers, according to the scientific Utopians, a fool's paradise of old-fashioned social values to the brutal, naked, neutral, egalitarian, objective fact of mechanical law. On the other hand, the idealistic Utopias from Brook Farm to William Morris and beyond attack the problem from a psychological basis and accuse the bourgeoisie violently for having sold the world into the cruel harem of the machine god. But the idealistic Utopias have been palpably unable to deliver the world from its captivity; their protests against the machine have been silenced like the song of a nightingale by a passing train.

The machine, as we know it in the West, is capital, and it is the peculiarity of capital to breed more capital through investment of profits; but in the scientific Utopias investment policy is regulated not by considerations which further a blind growth of the capitalistic avalanche, but by considerations of public welfare. The modern world, unbalanced by a persistent dearth of meaning, a society which smashes the unity of creation in order to use the energies derived from artificial distinctions in the service of private and public imperialisms, is supposed to make way for a functional whole whose problem is to keep its bulk in balance on a fixed territorial basis. That the air has changed in a world of closed frontiers everybody has noticed since the great depression started; this does not mean that instincts have changed.

The paths of power lead through the elysium of monopoly. What we witness today is a change in the character of monopoly, from the naïve exploitation of foreign markets, which Lenin called the "final stage of capitalism," to the more sophisticated national and international cartellization of capital and labor. "The new elites," writes Mr. Burnham, "will be managers instead of bourgeois." [16] A return to a kind of medieval

## UTOPIAS WITHOUT SPIRIT 157

guild system, with the mentality of the power age instead of the mentality of the Middle Age, haunts the imagination of our progressive writers, who for that matter are not necessarily socialists. To anybody with eyes to see, the recession of the tide of individualism that had its origin in the Renaissance has begun; money, the invisible army which conquers for the individual the key positions in the social organism, changes high command and becomes an instrument manipulated under public control in the interest of function. The conservative magazine *Time*, in a survey of "business in 1942," reports "an actual redistribution of income from owners to employees." This does not worry *Time*, because the businessman's reward was "not income but a key place in the national effort." Thus in the very stronghold of laissez-faire, in peace and war, something comparable to the organic aspect of the Middle Ages is indeed emerging, a new hierarchy based on function instead of possession; but this is only a superficial similarity, because this new "managerial" society is anything but static.

If we turn from the scientific Utopias which have not yet been tried to the liberal and totalitarian realities which have been tried, we observe that they were successful because they were dynamic and not stationary; they were lit up with all the panics, storms, and improvisations that power-craze and superstitions have projected into human history from the beginning of time. And the machine, far from exercising a neutralizing and "scientific" influence, has only aggravated with its boundless energies the irrationality of the spectacle. Liberalism offered countless opportunities for individual approaches to the alluring fairyland of power and prestige through the medium of money. While people only a few years ago were inclined to believe that the "spiral of prosperity" would rise without end, in proportion to the rising of man's intelligence and industry, we are now inclined to believe that the success of laissez-faire economy was a specific phase in world history, dependent on the possibilities of expansion of which the harnessing and allocation of America's untapped energies was paramount. With this expansion checked, the rubbing of the Aladdin's lamp of laissez-faire failed to produce satisfactory results. The liberal myth also failed to fire the victims of depression emotionally, as it had the soldiers in Valley Forge. To do that, it had to be attacked. The desiccation of the roots of dynamism and the ensuing indecision as to the course which ought to be taken made people in liberal countries, before the second world war started, suddenly doubt the wisdom of the last hundred and fifty years.

The liberal reality paled before the totalitarian reality for the very reason that the latter was a new and more drastic kind of dynamism. The power age was like a tree which, without a sun to give it an integrating impulse, would collapse and crush the people it sheltered. When the sun that so far had provided warmth refused to rise, people invented artificial suns. The totalitarian realities lived by the artificial fires which their various attacks against the liberal reality kindled. They did not promise "individual prestige through money power," but following the recipe of Georges Sorel, they certainly provided powerful myths which made the man in the street to a certain extent willing to bear his privations. There have been myths before; but the modern myths are dynamic, not static. As the expressionistic wood dwellers found out, a static myth that is successful in the machine age still has to be found. And, whether they like it or not, on this, and not on a technical "lessening of man," depends the success of the scientific Utopias.

Walter Lippmann says in the *Good Society* [17] that all collectivism, whether it be communist or fascist, is military in method, in purpose, in spirit, and can be nothing else. The "managerial society" into which the countless private concerns of the laissez-faire society are slowly, or rather rapidly blending, is a collectivism too; if Mr. Lippmann's definition is right (presumably it is meant to be right only for the machine age), then managerial society cannot sail ahead without a generous breeze of militant temper. In fact, we know of no collectivism in the machine age which has functioned outside protest and counter-protest. Mr. Burnham throws the managers of every creed and color—"Fascist or Leninist or Stalinist or New Dealers or Technocratic"—into the same pot and warns us to have no illusions about their ideologies. More than ten years ago G. H. Soule, in his introduction to the etiquette of planning,[18] wrote the dangerously Goebbelsian sentence: "Ardent faith in something, no matter whether that something is objectively true in all its details or not, does occasionally move mountains." Like Trotsky, Mr. Soule wants to move mountains collectively, but unlike Trotsky he has his doubts whether anything but war will bring people into the emotional state where they drop their customary inhibitions before the impossible.

While the liberal world, on the rocks since 1929, has been looking for a task aside from war that might galvanize the energies idle since the close of the age of expansion, Nazism got its dynamic start by making a huge bonfire not only of a few books, but of the celestial city which has sustained the imagination of Europe before the advent of the bourgeois. The celestial city had been interpreted by the middle class in such a way that it seemed to disillusioned, disinherited, untutored, and resentful people just like bourgeois timidity, pretence, opium, and an excuse for doing nothing.

We must say it again and again: Over the gate that leads into the machine age is written, EVERYTHING FOR DYNAMISM. Next to the entrance there is also a sign, STATIC DISPOSITIONS NEED NOT APPLY. If these are the prerequisites governing the selection of the human type desirable for the machine age, one can perhaps understand a doctrine of accelerated immoral evolution and permanent disaster; but one cannot see how Utopias which proclaim the end of evolution and a stationary social engineering can have a chance of survival. Yet the future of the human species depends on the combination of the machine, which so far is used for the sake of dynamic expansion, and a static society, which should use the machine for spiritual experiences, for which, however, no psychological basis exists after one hundred and fifty years of middle-class reign.[19]

## CHAPTER V

# THE CENTURY OF THE COMMON MAN

> ...the thousand-headed masses
> That moved with mystery grow
> beautiful.
> —STEFAN GEORGE [1]

> All things live in a depth, where there are no secrets—because they live with each other and in each other. Only we have placed ourselves outside the world. We burned all bridges and bondages behind us. The really superior man would be he who would forget that he is man. Our spirit and wit should be employed to give us back that feeling of the world which the other things possess in their unconsciousness.
> —ELIZABETH OF AUSTRIA

SALAS Y GOMEZ WAS ONLY A VERY UNATTRACTIVE BARE spot; in order to survive on it, and to fan the biochemical compound of bones and humidity with which he was entrusted into a fire that burned with sweet rewarding flames, its only inhabitant had to practise "lessening of man." All that had happened to the young man before he landed on Salas y Gomez was pre-history so far as he was concerned.

His real history began when his argument with the Whole started—Job's great argument; but he became himself only when the history of this argument ended, when the royal hunter, the Whole, had slain the leviathan of the individual you. I believe with the Marxists that everything we have so far called history is in reality pre-history, and that history begins when it ends, when the consciousness of the Unconditioned supplants the insufficient consciousness of individual man.

To say good-bye to history or pre-history would be the same as saying good-bye to the spells of the surface which so far have integrated the fragments of the Occident against each other. It is like the man on Salas y Gomez turning from his resentment and the weakness of his physical condition to the one thing left to him, besides the actuality of his body: the slow cryptic power of the deep talking in him, shaping his thoughts, opening perspectives and a succession of relations and meanings, and a synthesis of suns and seasons, and an infinite analogy of death and resurrection. It is Gandhi turning from practical politics, which St. Augustine called a thieves' den, to his ashram and the exercises of Satyagraha—impractical politics which are ever so much more efficient than practical politics and which the "dumb Michel" would have done well to emulate.

We can rest assured, however, that his good-bye to the superficial, the spatializing ego, will not be uttered by occidental lips if it can be helped. The Occident is surface glorified; without surface it is not Occident. The exotic and tragic beauty of human weaknesses—lust, pride, luxury, vengeance, bravery, defiance, and covetousness—is its domain. But occidental history can be divided into two periods: In the first, Europeans sinned picturesquely; in the second, their sins have become ugly. Today Europeans have lost their perspective for their bad behaviour; their pride and rapacity, which once created sublime counterpoises and the catharsis of a noble expression, have become unutterably one-sided and total. Their bad behavior—out of which Dante made his *Commedia*, and Shakespeare his tragedies, and the Venetians their pictures, carnivals, and seductions, and the Frenchmen their thoughts, harmonies, and grandeurs, and the Germans their mystic folklore, exuberant Baroque, and boundless dirges—is no longer fertile; the suffering it causes is infernal, and not of the kind that pays in heaven. André Gide spoke once of a letter he received from a doctor during the first world war; the doctor, referring to wounded soldiers, wrote, "If they could only conceive of their suffering as a sacrifice." The suffering of Europe is dumb and senseless, it is without rhyme, it no longer belongs in the book of human fate, just as certain poems, written after an author has become insane, do not form an organic part of his works.

This is the bare, desolate rock, not in the Pacific, but in cold black infinity. Ever since Copernicus removed the planet Earth from the heart of the Deity and made it a third-rate tributary of the Sun, and Newton murdered with the prose of his gravitation formula the super-reality mankind was wont to lodge between the endless possibilities of constellations; ever since Darwin robbed man of ancestry straight from the hands of God, and Marx made the digestive apparatus the tabernacle towards which the historical process moved—ever since all these devastating truths have been unearthed, the protestation of the seriousness of the biological fact called Man should have become more and more difficult. But lo and behold, on the contrary, the more mankind became convinced that its individual specimens were nothing but aggregates of certain chemicals whose market value, after careful segregation, would amount to not more than ninety cents in American currency—the more mankind arrived at these matter-of-fact conclusions—the more store it set paradoxically by the conditions under which the aggregates were likely to prosper. And the less became the distance to its weaknesses.

These weaknesses, institutionalized, were pampered; solid and overwhelming, they denounced doubt of their supreme validity or suggestion of their vanity as high treason. This is what explains the fate of art and the travesty of religion during the nineteenth century. The frenzy of individual climbing, local climbing, regional climbing, national climbing, racial climbing, climbing on a continental scale—take it away and there is nothing in the world today to defend man's high opinion of himself against the insignificance of his station in Eternity.

And yet, this "nothing" is what we face. In spite of pathetic excesses of philistine pride, which blocked the *actus purus* of genuine creation, the "lessening of man" made inexorable progress on the physical plane until it culminated in the mechanical extermination of millions of human beings in two world wars. The bareness of the rock on which we live became horribly and shamelessly visible; our distinctions and differences lost their dignity in the light of the revelations from Copernicus to Marx, and became as light as a feather to a consciousness which becomes increasingly adjusted to our smallness. "In the vastness of creation we dare not claim for any one thing precedence over any other," writes Professor Alexander. Under the aspect of a greater reality, the Universe and Eternity, one human obsession is as good as any other, and in any case does not amount to much. More and more, Universe and Eternity are imposing themselves from day to day upon our consciousness, as human space and human time dwindle. In this connection the Hitlerian obsession, to mention only the most conspicuous, was, to use the words of Talleyrand, worse than a crime, it was a stupidity.

There is absolutely no reason why the century of the common man, which we have entered, should not achieve the goal of keeping alive in tolerable comfort an enormous number of the human species. This tremendous achievement is really not a triumph but the outcome of a renunciation—the acceptance of man's obliteration so far as the motives of his history go. In order that security may be granted to the human species, history has to stop rocketing human meteors into the firmament of action. The spontaneity of the human race must not find expression any longer through the medium of the politico-historical clay. Pericles and Bismarck vanish before the temporary bureaucratic excellence of a scrubwoman. The style of the imposing hall of reason into which mankind is now entering would be polluted by such ornamental hangovers, deriving from special revelations and specific loyalties. Their relativity is exposed.

It indeed looks as if the wisest course to take under the circumstances would be to accept the bareness of the rock. The engineers of planned Utopias implore us to accept it. They implore us to accept it in the interest of the security of the life force which uses the shape of man for its unfathomable ends. The machine age insures the survival of the life force with its two billion human heads on the bare rock, the globe, as the birds' eggs insured the survival of the life force with its one head on the bare rock Salas y Gomez. Each year the mileage of pipe lines and tubes and air transport will increase; but this happy development of technical facilities will no longer do the "richer members of the community a great deal of good." So far as mankind is concerned, there is only one particular left, and that is its totality. Man cannot any longer escape the Unconditioned, he cannot any longer escape Truth, if Truth means emancipation from relativity.

All this is sensationally expressed by Walt Whitman, the American Poseidon who, with his unconditioned trident, shakes the many specific waters and rivulets of human conceit. "One Identity, One Identity—I reject nothing," cried Whitman. But here comes D. H. Lawrence, the European "bored beyond sustenance" by the twilight of the demons.

"This is machine," he groans. "Only matter does not make any distinctions, matter gravitates because it is helpless and mechanical, man is man because he selects."

Lawrence [2] pitted against Whitman's indiscriminate enthusiasm for the indiscriminate his own dark, particular obsessions, the call from the deep. "ONE DIRECTION! whoops America, and sets off . . . in an automobile. ALLNESS! shrieks Walt at a crossroad, going whizz over an unwary Red Indian. ONE IDENTITY! chants democratic En Masse, pelting behind in motor cars, oblivious of the corpses under the wheels." The corpses are the tribal gods, Teutonic, Jewish, American-Indian, Indian, African. Identity is machine, protests Lawrence, Allness is empty, an addled egg. Either you go back to your demon, or you cease to be man.

Well, if this is the choice, we prefer to cease to be man. We prefer no meaning at all to the demoniac meaning of D. H. Lawrence, which Goebbels switched on whenever he needed something to make his combination of barracks and factories furiously active. Lawrence's rebellious demons ought to be buried with Hitler. Logically, the coming years of peace ought to begin with the funeral of life's delight in particularization. This would be all right with the planners of up-to-date Utopias. The crude, unredeemed, biological fact out of which man emerged, the original stuff of man, the common clay of our prehistoric beginnings, asks nothing better than being canalized into harmless patterns by self-imposed mechanical controls, with history, properly speaking, at an end. History was Man acting out freely his destiny, his differences, his "demon"—post-history is man's voluntary return into the original, prehistorical identity of the species.

If this is better than the war of D. H. Lawrence's demons against each other, it is nevertheless defeat. We have maintained all through this book, and we say it here for the last time: The only means to turn this defeat, which in a sense is inevitable, into victory, and to make a self-confinement of mankind in a world-wide productive plant psychologically bearable, is to accept "lessening of man" not as a calculated premise for man's comfort, but as a *sacrifice* which is necessary for the unhindered operation of the cosmic firebird, Spirit, in the heart of Time. Without the acknowledgment that not man but a superhuman inspiration is the A and O, the breath and entelechy, the only real purpose and queen bee of our organization, the colony of human bees on the lonely rock is doomed. "Man must abandon himself," said Pascal, "in order not to be abandoned."

Once upon a time sophistication was faced with that residue of innocence, the believing people. "To go into the people" was in Russia a term for "to turn one's back on the unbelieving Westerner." Dostoevsky, at the climax of his famous oration in honor of Pushkin, donned the garb of the common man as if it had been the robe of a high priest. "The people is the body of God." The great secret was whispered from one toiling generation to the next that Christ had been poor. Pope John XXII threatened with the stake anybody who dared to entertain so dangerous a notion. The anonymous masses were the roses in the cathedral of mankind through which floated the light that shamed the eager candles of the clever. Their toil rolled on like a river—"la marée mystique des pauvres" [3]— the mystic tide of the poor, the mystic and innocent bridegrooms of poverty, ever repudiating the temptor, and ever accepting their fate. It is the roundabout way to results which they fear, and the detour to harmony which they cherish. Chuang-tze tells the story of the gardener who refuses to use a contraption that would help him get water from the well: If I employ a machine, he said, I am bound to do my job like a machine; by doing my job like a machine, my heart too will soon be like a machine.

Poverty was to Joachim of Flora an invitation to the Holy Ghost to dwell in our midst—the Holy Ghost of whom Shaw [4] said incomparably in our time that, while it was formerly the most nebulous person in the Trinity, it is now its sole survivor as it has always been its real unity. Joachim of Flora and the Franciscans celebrate the meeting between poverty and the Holy Ghost, to call nothing one's own but one's song—"Qui vere monachus est nihil reputat esse suum nisi citharam." Karl Buecher [5] collected hundreds of songs echoing the divine animation that springs forth daily under a thousand different skies—songs which people used to sing during the ceremony we call work. Chinese peasants, moving into the mountains every morning to gather tea, sang a hymn in honor of their enterprise, which they compared to a pilgrimage to the Western paradise. The Volga boatmen "accepted the universe," and the women of Madagascar acted, when they cultivated the ricefields, like bayaderes trying to please a god.

Miguel Covarrubias,[6] in his book on Bali, describes the bandjars, or co-operative societies as we would call them in our dry idiom; they watched the magic of work unfold with proper art and majesty in their Indonesian Eden; when night fell they sent the arpeggios to their tireless orchestras through fragrant vales because demons and darkness recommended a change of expression; but whether playing the gamelangs, or ploughing, or reaping, or feasting, the cardinal consideration was always to "dance with the gods." In his *Mutual Help* Kropotkin—who, if he had known of the Balinese bandjar, would have had a priceless illustration for his thesis—quotes a medieval ordinance which insists that "everybody must be pleased with his work."

The medieval fraternities of workers in Flanders and Lyons, toiling in the frozen music of crepuscular cities, rolled the stone from the tomb of their narrow space; their triumph over the refractory material of the world was not mere routine, but was understood by them in its vast metaphysical connotations. Work interpreted as spiritual discipline gave these people a superhuman patience, detachment from results.

Their days came to them as a curtain rises over an esoteric theatre where not only men speak, and animals, but inanimate objects too, as they do in van Gogh's pictures. Their daily work spoke in a great chorus whose rhythm put dead things into flower, as Joseph's stick flowered when he met Mary. They had reached the stage where not they worked, but their inspiration worked through them.

Here we touch upon a great and beautiful secret, one I wish I could linger on. The inspiration was not theirs. They had, in the famous phrase, found themselves because they had lost themselves. The ideal worker—in order to meet him one has to travel to the East where the Middle Ages are still alive in places—did not "multiply distinctions." He was unable to leave the orbit of the central impulse, which is a mysterious overflow. One might call it the spontaneity of the Demiurge reaching from heaven to hell, connecting all things, a spontaneity the worker is called upon to match. The ideal worker is prisoner of his heavenly appointed duty to rescue the objects he touches from death—a good surface of paint on a door is as truly an emotional or aesthetic consideration as significant form. The ideal worker is a prisoner of freedom well-comprehended, a prisoner of an inward direction whose beginning and end we do not know, the prisoner perhaps of a playful god whom Master Eckhart defines: a thing welling up in itself, pouring any part of itself into any other part before it runs forth and bubbles over without—"like a horse turned loose in a lush meadow."

I have seen doors as blue or red as if the god of Eckhart had poured the blue and red into them, or as well-carved as if the god "turned loose in a lush meadow" had carved them. "God walks amongst the pots and pipkins," wrote Santa Teresa, and this is the beautiful secret. There is a point where Martha is Mary, systole is diastole, Sabbath the day of labor, "and man's activity is drawn into his inwardness." [7] His inwardness never ceases; he does not break it down through his activity, he builds it up. But so does matter bear the impact of his inwardness. Without man's inwardness, matter would be lost. What is meant by this becomes clear if we accept for a moment with Bergson that "life makes itself," in contrast to matter, which "unmakes itself." Matter is an inversion of the life current; life constitutes an energy which remounts the steps which matter descends. The creation, as matter, is an energy which exhausts itself; life is an interruption, a reversal of this process of degradation. But by life is not meant the multiplier of distinctions. Life in this context is not a demon-obsessed biological stuff, a material alive which merely adds to the material that "unmakes itself" and that, because it suffers, as it were, from the state of chaos out of which it cannot lift itself by its own power, is directed towards dissolution as the only possible solution. By life is meant a possible manifestation of inwardness, an "eternity alive," a translation into actuality of the most un-actual thing imaginable from the point of view of finality, of the "Here and Now" that cannot die or, in Bergson's terms, of the original energy which preceded the phase of degradation.

Life, as an actualization of the self-love of matter in the jaws of degradation, adds to the chaos. But life as an actualization of the "Nunc Aeternum," of the mystic "Here and Now," of a flash of genius sustained through all Eternity beyond the degradation of matter, adds to the cosmos. The ideal worker—and there were times when all workers naïvely could not help being ideal—projected his inwardness into the matter and thus stopped its degradation. He participated in the *poiesis*, the making, art and creation which opposes the "unmaking" of matter. Like the peasant in Breughel's "Icarus," or the "peasant saint" of whom Carlyle speaks in *Sartor Resartus*—"he that must toil outwardly for the lowest of man's wants, is also toiling inwardly for the highest"—or the Iranian laborers in that most solemn of Goethean invocations, "Legacy of Old-Persian Faith," he, the ideal worker, works in a kind of God-given trance such as Adam was in when his rib produced Eve.

The believing people—that is, life participating through inwardness in the cosmos—used to cure, with lamb-like patience, the anarchy caused by those who participated in the degradation of matter. The sublime processes of believing people, the unending purge of matter, the spiritualization of the good earth through man, and the spiritualization of man through the answers of the good earth, this mute, almost unperceived, anonymous process of the people—anonymous like the cathedrals which, in stone images right and left of their entrances, celebrate labor as the discipline that breeds not only fruits of the earth but fruits of the spirit—this regenerating, spontaneous, tragic, and beautiful process has left the earth. The people, the great corrective of sophistication, have left the earth, because naïveté, the thousand oracles arising out of Nature's divine unconcern, has left the earth. The people refuse to be naïve any longer, and we cannot blame them, because naïveté, instead of being understood—in the days when the people were the "body of the Lord"—as a sibylline guidance of human destiny, has become in bourgeois civilization a social liability. It has become the mark of simpletons, of "dumb Michels." The people, egged on by Marx, shed naïveté like a worthless old skin; the people became smart, smarter indeed than the bourgeoisie, which is forced to surrender its scepter, though not, as Péguy pointed out so poignantly, its mentality.

In the century of the common man everybody will be bourgeois. Everybody will anticipate the rewards which are really reserved to inwardness and spontaneity, everybody will travel on short cuts to these rewards, because it will be a calculated century. The people, the fountain and revelation of Life's very own undiluted moods, will be covered up; they will remember their former pristine ways with shame. I remember how often, when I was in Asia, feasting on the perfumed cakes and honeyed wafers of its spiritual arcana, I was proudly offered the "ersatz" with which the Orient thought it could buy the admiration of the West: street cars, neon signs, and guns.

But Eternity is not stopped or blacked out by street cars, neon signs, or guns, or by bourgeois or philistines or Hitler either, or by you or by me. The total fact of Eternity, the total fact of Existence, is not affected by our actions; but our actions are affected by whether we know how to meet the total fact in what we do, as the ideal worker did instinctively. The century of the common man starts now; but when will it end?

Sir James Jeans[8] gives us an idea of the amount of time we still have to spend after the victory of the common man and the unification of the world through the machine. Take a postage stamp and let its thickness represent about five thousand years, the time it has taken the recorded history of the conscious human being to unfold. Then take postage stamps, each representing about five thousand years, and pile them upon each other until the height of the pile equals the height of Mont Blanc—such is the time during which the earth will remain habitable. Sir James's figure is a million million, or a trillion, years.

For all practical purposes the century of the common man will never end; it is eternal. On the other hand, the space into which this never-ending century is permitted to crowd its inventions and manifestations, its smiles and terrors, is so small that already, when the eternity of the common man is still in its embryonic stage, the human ant, if it is in a jet plane, can shoot around the arena in a few dozen hours. And this arena will never expand.

The common man, whose apotheosis marks the end of an infinitesimally short prelude called human history, is about to become the hero of an acrobatic act whose duration is practically unlimited. His success will require a true understanding of the difficult art of living—more than understanding that men are not mere human particulars organized into resentful masses. His success will require detachment from the moment and its vanity, and development of natural affinity to the deeper memories of the species. His success will require the balancing of an infinitely small amount of space with an infinitely great amount of time. The common man steps into the arena totally unprepared for this difficult performance. The bourgeoisie has bequeathed him an intellect which multiplies distinctions in limited space; but the intuitions through which unlimited time presses toward inward unity have been ignored as the Jews ignored the Messiah.

The oppressive fixedness of our spatial existence is alleviated by political and scientific rearrangements of our external environment—a necessary, sometimes salutary, sometimes disastrous proceeding, whose crises are represented by nothing less than world wars. In order to prepare a bed of roses for our spatial existence we must paradoxically resign ourselves to the fact that we cannot win the freedom we are longing for through the means of space. The only freedom we can hope for is the development of our consciousness in Time.

Can we not already imagine ourselves retiring into "oases of time" [9]—millions of little white sanitary cubic or igloo-shaped habitations dotting the globe as hermitages or neighborhood units, broad-acre cities, Iona communities, *Cités Universitaires*, and smokeless biocentric communal bodies of glass and plastic, revolving around work, which as a mode employed for results, breaks the Universe apart, but as a function expresses it? But more important than work outside is work inside—the cells of the neighbourhood units will resemble the one in which Prospero dissolved the meaningless necessity of space into the meaningful freedom of a dream. These oases of time (and what is time but an eternity of potentialities?) will choose as their motto not the anarchic-optimistic maxim of

Rabelais and the Karamasovs, "Do as you will"; but, let us hope, they will write over their gates the beautiful aphorism that is recorded from a Byzantine emperor, "We gained the whole world and threw its shell behind us, so that we might keep its core."

Perhaps our judgment of the bourgeois world, the hothouse in which empires and resentment, monopolies and complacency thrive, has been too harsh. At last we see meaning in the process of the ice age down the slope of the last one hundred and fifty years. Without the complete control of all available quantity, no schemes which had quality through abnegation as their centre had a real chance. Quantity boisterously entered the front door, while quality begged for a crust of bread at the servant's entrance. Now, after quantity has had its day, let us pray that the victory of the common man does not mean the perpetuation of a merciless resentment, but rather that we—or the common man, which is the same thing— will now proceed to make the environment yield to the overwhelming pressure of an infinite amount of time that longs to become quality in our consciousness. The future predominance of such laboratories of the inner life is the real justification for the predominance of laboratories in the interest of outward life in our day.

But "laboratory" is a bad term. We do not make time and eternity and the "brooding presence of the Whole"; they make us. Who can say what they hold for the future? What tunes will the bow of the Universe play on our consciousness? What mutations will appear in our physique? The appearance of the thumb, which made the development of our physical environment possible, presupposed the action of five senses; the *usnisa*, the protuberance that appeared on Buddha's head under the Bo-tree, presupposed enlightenment. What physical changes, what wings, what spontaneity of eyes, electricity of limbs, originality of heart, what angelic colors, what new expressiveness of gestures will accompany our attaining a sixth sense? Through what metamorphoses will our consciousness pass, what magic spectacles will make the drabness of a rainy day a disguised compliment from the Absolute? What ornamental habits will tie a meeting on Main Street to the One where everyone and everything is meeting here and now and always? In what Dumbarton Oaks shall we confer with the true powers of the Universe, in what San Francisco shall we sign treaties with the true processes of the world, after the formations of complacency and resentment have melted in the exigencies of a time that wants fulfillment in depth?

For the last time I shall quote Goethe. Goethe, like Chartres, belongs to the Europe that is not represented at Dumbarton Oaks, Bretton Woods, or San Francisco. The ruined space that is called Europe today, and that can be represented or condemned at international gatherings, ceased to be Europe long ago. It lived so long as the monuments and deeds of its elite had their source not in the conditions of man, moment, and necessity, but in the vast, deep, mysterious freedom of the Unconditioned, bending the engines of society to its mighty and inspiring sweep. Can we have any hope that the world as a whole will recover what Europe has lost? Will the pendulum of our destiny swing again into the neighbourhood of Grace? Here is what Goethe says: [10] "The century must come to our aid, Time must take the place of Reason, and an enlarged heart must exchange the lower for the higher advantage."

# NOTES

# NOTES

## INTRODUCTION

1. Jacques Maritain, *Art and Scholasticism*, New York, 1935.
2. The present study is blissfully unconcerned with epistemological problems. The extreme form of idealism which is the philosophy of these pages, is not advocated as a truth of description, but of appreciation, to use Royce's language; or, in William James's words, as a pragmatic truth: "That belief, the enactment of which is functionally efficacious, is truly efficacious." My belief in the efficacy of the mental strategy I am discussing is my own subjective experience. It so happens that this subjective experience, of which I shall say more in the third chapter, tallies with weighty testimonies of acknowledged but widely disregarded sages in favour of the contemplative life.

Can we definitely assert that, in a causal sense, spirit comes before matter, or matter comes before spirit, if we agree to a dualistic viewpoint at all? We read in O'Shaughnessy's "Ode": "We ... built Niniveh with our sighing, And Babel itself with our mirth." The mental state was first, the materialization second: "It is the soul that builds itself a body." (Schiller.) On the opposite pole M. R. Cohen asserts (in *Reason and Nature*): "If we bring about certain bodily states, we shall also have their mental accompaniments.... All education and the influencing of our fellow men depends upon choosing the right physical expression or means to bring about the desired mental state." Here the physical environment is first, and the corresponding mental state second. The point I am trying to make is that the "desired mental state" is the end towards which both the individual constitution and the constitution of the human world should aim. If bibles and symphonies are the flower of matter, then we should be able by proper arrangement to produce Beethoven and the prophets with the same accuracy as we can predict a solar eclipse. (The illustration is Bergson's.) Since bibles and symphonies are, however, pieces of spontaneity and finding them in the vast necessity of matter is the big surprise the cosmos holds for us, it is difficult to see how we can adequately evaluate the freedom of the spirit in terms of material necessity.

My own experience is that I was unhappy in times of affluence and that in times of poverty I was unhappy too; that is I was always unhappy when I saw the style of my life dependent on the style of my environment. According to the tradition of idealistic philosophy happiness consists in over-coming this dependence. The social accident caused so many tempests in the teacup of the modern world that it might be advisable to diminish the importance which it holds in contemporary imagination by a study of Chuang-tze, especially Book II; of the *Tao Te Ching;* of the *Bhagavad Gita;* and of the Fourth Gospel and the Epistle to the Romans.

3. Pitirim Sorokin, *The Crisis of our Age*, New York, 1941.
4. Cf. Ananda Coomaraswamy, *The Transformation of Nature in Art*, 1935.
5. Maritain, *op. cit.*, p. 166.
6. Cf. *Meister Eckhart*, translated by Raymond Bernard Blakney, 1941.
7. For the understanding of this introduction, and as a matter of fact of the whole book, it is necessary to recall here a certain commonplace of Indian thought. As the best approach for a layman like myself to this thought I recommend several penetrating essays by Ananda Coomaraswamy, especially *Hinduism and Buddhism* (1944); *Philosophy, East and West* (ed. Charles A. Moore, 1944); Rudolf Otto, *Mysticism East and West* (transl., New York, 1932); and C. E. M. Joad, *Counter Attack From the East* (London, 1933). Easily accessible is Lin Yutang's selection of original writings in *The Wisdom of China and India* (New York, 1942). The Chinese variant of the problem is discussed in the classic volume by Marcel Granet, *La Pensée Chinoise* (1934). It is no paradox that a particular person arriving at his fulfillment ceases being a particular person and a particular consciousness. In order to fulfill ourselves we have to "die to ourselves." The self becomes the Self (with a capital S). The hero of *Salas y Gomez* is born twice: first empirically, second spiritually. Through the second birth, which is at the same time a dying to himself, he is

raised into the spiritual equivalent of the paradise, namely the Whole, where things no longer are divided but connected. Atman and Brahman have become One.

In all major philosophies the essence of truth is held to be the self-transcendence of the individual. Kant regarded the moral law as self-imposed by the rational will of man, who became a person because he ceased to depend on outward authority; but the inward authority to which he turned was no longer himself, but a universal, the moral law.

The difficulty, to which A. O. Lovejoy has devoted a searching study (*The Great Chain of Being*, Cambridge, Mass., 1936), is the reconciliation of this philosophy, whose goal is the end of the particular ("God has no style, His idiosyncrasy is Being") with the apparent intention of the Cosmos to become as particularized and diversified as possible. It will become clear as the book proceeds that we think the main problem left to man at this stage of his evolution is to reconcile in himself the two conflicting trends. We believe that this reconciliation can only be effected if man makes his expression in space a symbol not of the harassing moment but of creative time, the "moving image of Eternity."

8. Maurice Magre, *Magicians, Seers and Mystics*, 1932, p. 259.

9. Cf. Mme. Alexandra David-Neel, *Initiations and Initiates in Tibet*, 1931, and *Magic and Mystery in Tibet*, 1932.

10. In Kuerschner's *Deutsche National Litteratur*, CVIII, 42.

# CHAPTER I

1. Virginia Woolf, *Roger Fry*, New York, 1940.
2. Mario Praz, *Romantic Agony*, New York, 1933.
3. Ernst Juenger, *Der Arbeiter*, Hamburg, 1932, p. 24.
4. Georges Bernanos, *Lettre aux Anglais*, Rio de Janeiro, 1942.
5. D. H. Lawrence.
6. Mary Austin, *The American Rhythm*, New York, 1923.
7. Vachel Lindsay, "On the Building of Springfield."
8. Baker Brownell and F. L. Wright, *Architecture and Modern Life*, New York, 1937.
9. *Commonweal*, 1943.
10. Gustave Thibon, *L'Inégalité, Facteur d'Harmonie*, 1939,

quoted in Francis Stuart Campbell, *The Menace of the Herd*, 1943.

11. Three other classic statements of the same thought are Ulysses' "degree" speech in *Troilus and Cressida*, I, iii; Chapter 18 of the *Bhagavad Gita;* and Chapter 12 of the Epistle to the Romans.

12. René Bazin, *The Coming Harvest*, quoted in *The World's Great Catholic Literature*, ed. G. N. Shuster, New York, 1942.

13. Charles Péguy, *Basic Verities*, New York: Pantheon Books, Inc., 1943, p. 81. Quoted by permission of the publisher.

14. Arthur Bryant, *Pageant of England*, New York and London, 1941, p. 107.

15. Max Eastman, "The Marxian Philosophy," *The Making of Society*, ed. V. F. Calvertin, 1937.

16. G. A. Borgese, *Goliath, The March of Fascism*, 1937.

17. The term "decomposed time" is made up in analogy to the Augustinian definition of time as "decomposed eternity"; cf. the discussion of the negative and positive aspect of time in N. Berdyaev, *Solitude and Society*, 1939, pp. 129 ff.

18. H. N. Wieman, *Normative Psychology of Religion*, New York, 1935.

19. In *Freedom*, ed. by Ruth Nanda Anshen, 1940.

20. Benjamin Kidd, *Principles of Western Civilization*, 1902.

21. *Basic Verities*, p. 87.

22. T. E. Hulme, in a University of Washington Chapbook (ed. H. Read), compares words with caterpillars: there are naked caterpillars which just crawl from one position to another—they are like a "flat word passed over the board like a counter"; and there are hairy caterpillars—"the hair is the vision the poet sees behind it." The truths about the world are either naked and definite, and then they probably are not true, or they have a conciliatory and indefinite halo about them. In a book that deals with the world as prose and the world as imagination, philosophy has offered no more welcome amplification of concepts than the splitting up of time into alarm-clock time and duration, and of truth into truth of description and truth of appreciation, and of knowledge into concepts by postulation and concepts by intuition.

23. Thomas Mann, *Buddenbrooks*, New York: Alfred A.

Knopf, Inc., 1929, p. 393. Quoted by permission of the publisher.
24. Stefan Zweig, *World of Yesterday*, New York, 1943.
25. Franz Werfel, "Not the Murderer," in *Twilight of a World*, New York, 1937, p. 690.
26. Alfred Mansfield Brooks, *From Holbein to Whistler*, New Haven, 1920.
27. Jules Lemaitre in Charles Maurras, *Enquête sur la Monarchie*, Paris, 1925.
28. T. S. Eliot, "Baudelaire in our Times," in *Essays Ancient and Modern*, New York, 1932.
29. Lionel Trilling, *E. M. Forster*, Norfolk, Conn.: New Directions, 1943, p. 28. Quoted by permission of the publisher.
30. Joseph de Maistre.

## CHAPTER II

1. The term "kairos" is amply discussed in Paul Tillich, *The Interpretation of History*, New York, 1936, pp. 129 ff.
2. N. Berdyaev, *The Russian Revolution*, 1932.
3. Peter F. Drucker, *The Future of Industrial Man*, New York, 1942.
4. C. J. Bulliett, *Significant Moderns and their Pictures*, 1936.
5. Quoted in P. H. Boynton, *Literature and American Life*, 1936.
6. Van Wyck Brooks, "The Sargasso Sea," in *Three Essays on America*, 1934.
7. Waldo Frank, *Re-discovery of America*, 1929.
8. Mary Austin, *The American Rhythm*, 1923.
9. G. Santayana, *Reason in Religion*, quoted in *The Philosophy of Santayana*, Evanston and Chicago, 1940, p. 468.
10. Margaret Anderson, *My Thirty Years' War*, 1930.
11. Thomas Craven, *Modern Art*, 1934.
12. I translated this from a German quotation in T. G. Masaryk, *Zur Russischen Geschichts-und Religionsphilosophie*, Jena, 1913, II, 218. The same quotation is rendered differently in Nicolas Berdyaev, *Leontiev*, London, 1940.
13. Matthew Arnold, *Culture and Anarchy*, London, 1869, p. 20.

14. William James, *The Will to Believe*, 1898, p. 168.
15. Cf. Leo Shestov, *La Nuit de Gethsémané*, Paris, 1924.
16. Lewis Mumford. Cf. "A Brief Outline of Hell," in *The Culture of Cities*, 1938, pp. 272 ff., for a discussion of the fateful relationship between defective social esthetics and defective social ideologies.
17. Denis de Rougemont, *Love in the Western World*, New York, 1940.
18. *Kunst und Kuenstler*, VI, 178.
19. F. W. Coker, *Recent Political Thought*, 1934.
20. Karl Loewenstein, in *Governments of Continental Europe*, ed. James T. Shotwell, New York, 1940, p. 446.
21. Quoted after Matthew Josephson, *Jean-Jacques Rousseau*, 1931.
22. Quoted from E. K. Rand, *Founders of the Middle Ages*, 1928.
23. Harry Elmer Barnes, *An Intellectual and Cultural History of the Western World*, 1941, p. 263.
24. Paul Verlaine, *Poems*, translated by Gertrude Hall, Chicago, 1895.
25. Plotinus, *Enneads*, V, 12.
26. Evelyn Underhill, *Mysticism*, 1910.
27. Reinhold Schneider, *Das Inselreich*, Leipzig, 1936.
28. Doch im Erstarren such ich nicht mein Heil,
    Das Schaudern ist der Menschheit bestes Teil;
    Wie auch die Welt ihm das Gefuehl verteure,
    Ergriffen fuehlt er tief das Ungeheure.
    —*Faust*, Part II, I, v.

Looking around in the available *Faust* translations for a rendering of the passage in English, I was grieved to find its poetry gone and its sense perverted. In prose the meaning would be something like this: Finality to me has no salvation; To live Infinity's great shock is mankind's finest gift; However your awe is ruined by society, Seized to your depth, you tremble in the grandeur of the world.

29. Wyndham Lewis, *Time and Western Man*, New York: Harcourt, Brace & Co., 1928. Quoted by permission of the publisher.

NOTES TO PAGES 88-102    185

30. F. A. Swinnerton, *Georgian Scene*, 1934.
31. Henri Bergson, *Time and Free Will*, London, 1913, p. 237.
32. Cf. Chuang-tze, "On Levelling All Things," in *The Wisdom of China and India*, ed. Lin Yutang, p. 637. "Take, for instance, a twig and a pillar, or the ugly person and the great beauty, and all the strange and monstrous transformations. These are all levelled together by Tao."
33. A. N. Whitehead, *Science and the Modern World*, New York, 1925.
34. *Ibid.*, p. 280.
35. In *Phaedrus*. At the end of his instruction through Krishna, Arjuna says in the *Bhagavad Gita*, "My delusion is destroyed and I have regained my memory through thy grace." The theory that Anamnesis, memory, is the substratum of every creative education is expressed by Goethe (to Chancellor Mueller) in the following classic sentences: Whatsoever great, beautiful and significant comes our way should not be recaptured later by an outward device, like a quarry. On the contrary, it should enter from the start the fabric of our inward life, become one with it, help breed a new, improved self and so ever building and forming, live on and work in us. There is no past which one should desire to have back; there is only an eternal New which unfolds by means of the *past's enlarged elements*.
36. Walter Pater, *The Renaissance*, 1910, p. 124.
37. Sir James Jeans, *The Mysterious Universe*, 1930.
38. Hrabanus Maurus used to say that astronomy "flooded his heart with love." Cf. H. O. Taylor, *The Medieval Mind*, I, 224. Pascal once wrote: "Geometrical propositions become emotions, like memory and joy."
39. Bertrand Russel, *The Scientific Outlook*, 1931, p. 262.
40. Ernst Robert Curtius, *Deutscher Geist in Gefahr*, 1932.
41. Cf. the same thought religiously expressed, "... the Holy Ghost over the bent world broods with warm breast...."—Gerard Manly Hopkins, "God's Grandeur."
42. Wyndham Lewis, *op. cit.*, pp. 180, 181.
43. Oswald Spengler, *Der Untergang des Abendlandes* (60th ed., 1927), p. 48.

## CHAPTER III

1. Charles Baudelaire, "Le Dandy" in *Pages de Critique*, Paris, without date.
2. Quoted in F. W. Foerster, *Europe and the German Question*, 1940.
3. It is perfectly possible that I exaggerate in the heat of the argument the size of the paradise bird. After thinking it over, however, I still maintain that a spiritual world view was sought in the 1920's much more ardently in Germany than in any of the countries which are setting out to re-educate it. The irony of the matter is that you must have ardour in order to become an angel; but having ardour and not yet being an angel, you are apt to confuse heaven with hell.
4. I have in mind the prose version of reason, Blake's "Reasoning Power, An abstract objecting power that negatives everything ... like hoar frost, and a mildew ...," the originator of "machinery and commerce and war." The unattached reason of Socrates and Spinoza, on the other hand, is a means to "intellectual salvation."
5. Aurel Kolnai, *The War against the West*, 1938.
6. Blaise Cendrars, *Sutter's Gold*, 1926.
7. Stefan Zweig, *Sternstunden der Menschheit* (Am. ed., 1930).
8. Rainer Maria Rilke wrote in 1923: "Germany, in the year 1918 ... could have shamed and shaken the whole world through an act of deep sincerity and conversion. Through a visible, determined renunciation of her falsely developed prosperity—in a word: through that humility which would have been so completely in character with her spirit ... the lost trait of that humility which strikes one as so constructive in the drawings of Duerer ... [But] she wanted to act and come out clear and on top, instead, according to her inmost nature, of bearing and enduring and being ready for her miracle."—*Heart of Europe, An Anthology*, New York: L. B. Fischer, 1943, p. 549. Quoted by permission of *Twice a Year*.

## CHAPTER IV

1. From "In Memory of W. B. Yeats," *Poems*, New York: Random House, Inc., 1937. Quoted by permission of the publisher.
2. *Le Mystère de la Charité de Jeanne d'Arc*, New York: Pantheon Books, Inc., 1943. Quoted by permission of the publisher.
3. Cf. Hans Freyer, *Der Staat*, 1925, and *Machiavelli und die Lehre vom Handeln*, 1938. Very informative, because intelligent, is the description of the diabolic neutrality of the state-machine by the Nazi-jurist Carl Schmitt, *Der Leviathan*, 1938.
4. Schmitt, *op. cit.*, p. 82.
5. Quoted in André Gide, *Dostoevsky*, New York, 1923.
6. Wilhelm Dilthey, quoted in Max Scheler, *Die Ursachen des Deutschenhasses*.
7. James Darmestetter, *Les Prophètes d'Israel*.
8. Phyllis Ackerman, *Tapestry, the Mirror of Civilization*, 1933, p. 136.
9. Leon Roth, "Jewish Thought in the Modern World," in *The Legacy of Israel*, Oxford, 1928, p. 433.
10. Heinrich Hauser, *Battle against Time*, 1939.
11. D. H. Lawrence.
12. Stuart Chase, *Mexico*, 1931.
13. Quoted in S. N. Harper, *The Government of the Soviet Union*, 1937.
14. Quoted in René Fülöp Miller, *Geist und Gesicht des Bolschewismus*, 1926.
15. Edward Hallett Carr, *Conditions of Peace*, 1942.
16. James Burnham, *The Managerial Revolution*, 1941.
17. Walter Lippmann, *The Good Society*, Boston, 1937. In *The New Republic* of July 26, 1939, R. G. Tugwell wrote significantly: "The fact is that only War has up to now proved to be such a transcending objective that doctrine is willingly sacrificed for efficiency. This ought to reveal something of the qualifications an objective must have in order to induce the sacrifice of prejudice and self-regard."

18. G. H. Soule, *Planned Society*, 1932.
19. Bergson has stated the problem thus: "...la mystique appelle la méchanique...la méchanique exigerait une mystique...." (Freely translated: "A myth requires a machine—a machine requires a myth.") *Les Deux Sources de la Morale et de la Religion;* Paris, 1934, pp. 334, 335.

## CHAPTER V

1. Stefan George, *Poems*, New York: Pantheon Books, Inc., 1943. Quoted by permission of the publisher.
2. D. H. Lawrence, "Studies in Classic American Literature," in *The Shock of Recognition*, ed. Edmund Wilson, 1943.
3. Elie Faure.
4. In *Man and Superman*.
5. Karl Buecher, *Arbeit und Rhythmus*.
6. Miguel Covarrubias, *Island of Bali*, 1937, pp. 60 ff., 207.
7. Rudolf Otto, *Mysticism East and West*, 1932.
8. Sir James Jeans, *The Universe around Us*, 1929.
9. Lewis Mumford, *The Condition of Man*, 1944.
10. In *Wanderjahre*.

www.ingramcontent.com/pod-product-compliance
Lightning Source LLC
Chambersburg PA
CBHW030111010526
44116CB00005B/203